W9-AYJ-767

Incorporate The Road To Riches

Second Edition 2001

Publisher: Laughlin Associates, Inc.
2533 N. Carson Street
Carson City, Nevada, 89706
www.laughlinassociates.com

Copyrights: Laughlin Associates, Inc. 2001

ISBN: 0-9701520-0-0

Disclaimer

All that we do is submitted and performed with the understanding that we are not engaged in rendering legal, accounting or other such professional service. If legal advice or other expert assistance is required, the services of a person in those professions should be sought.

The information, ideas, and suggestions contained herein have been developed from sources including publications and research that are considered and believed to be reliable, but cannot be guaranteed insofar as they apply to any particular individual, corporation or taxpayer. Moreover, because of the technical nature of this material and the fact that laws and statutes are never static, but ever changing, the assistance of a competent, qualified lawyer or accountant is recommended when implementing the strategies discussed in this book.

Laughlin Associates, Inc., its employees, and agents specifically disclaim any liability, loss or risk, personal or otherwise, that is incurred as a consequence of the use and/or application of the information in this material.

DEDICATION

This book is dedicated to those who dare to strike out on their own and create their own opportunities. It is dedicated to the rare breed of people who take the risks, take the lead and take charge. It is dedicated to the extraordinary—the entrepreneur!

Lower Your Taxes, Secure Your Assets And Protect Your Loved Ones As You *"Incorporate And Grow Rich!"*

FORWARD

This book was written for people who wish to learn how to structure their business and personal affairs so that they are able to properly implement little known strategies. You are probably one of those people. This book can greatly reduce your personal liability in any enterprise, protecting your assets from the risk of lawsuits or judgments, provide you with a vehicle to obtain financial privacy, and reduce your taxes.

You will learn that it is not what you do in business, but how you do it, that determines the amount of success you ultimately enjoy.

These strategies, usually reserved for only the richest and most powerful, have been successfully used by thousands of small business people all across the country.

There are only three things that you must keep in mind when implementing any business strategy.

1. You must have a sound and legitimate business purpose for implementing the strategy.

2. You must completely document the purpose, the action and the timing of the strategy.

3. You must insure that all criteria necessary to allow you to implement the strategy are met and maintained.

It is our privilege to bring you this information and we look forward to helping you in any way we can in your pursuit of lower taxes, greater privacy and stronger asset protection.

You should never "buck city hall," as the saying goes. Instead, we believe (and strongly advocate) that everyone should be armed with the information that heretofore was solely the domain of the rich and powerful. Properly implemented, these strategies work and usually pay for themselves many times over from the multitude of benefits they can provide you.

CHAPTER 1
The Basics

CHAPTER 2
Your Corporate Strategy

CHAPTER 3
Summary

CHAPTER 4
Limited Liability Companies

INTRODUCTION

Incorporating represents an exciting opportunity for many to protect their personal assets from the perils that exist in doing business today. Incorporating is also an excellent way for many to gain substantial tax savings and many other benefits.

All you need to do is read the newspapers to determine that we live in a very dangerous environment for conducting business—or doing much of anything. The risk of getting sued today, especially when conducting your own business, is greater than it's ever been. There are now more practicing attorneys in the United States than anywhere else in the world. While the United States has barely 5% of the world's population, we have 70% of the world's lawyers. American attorneys work under a system which is not found anywhere else in the world, and that is the contingency fee system. Under the contingency fee rules, attorneys will file lawsuits without their clients having to put up any money. The successful attorney then takes a percentage of anything he is able to get from a defendant. This percentage, or contingency fee, will typically run in an area of 30% to 47% of everything that is collected. Is it any wonder then that attorneys press for very high awards in lawsuits? Only a few years ago, a jury award of a million dollars or more was unusual. Now, a jury award of a million dollars is the norm. Lawsuits are becoming more and more common, as a result making this a very dangerous climate in which to do business.

Incorporating your business is certainly a good answer to protect yourself from business lawsuits. You cannot wait until you've been notified of an impending lawsuit). The time to incorporate is while your legal seas are calm. In the following pages we will discuss the protection that incorporating can provide.

Another problem business people experience is ever increasing taxes. Sometimes it seems that just when you make a profit, the tax man is there to take it away from you. No one is required to pay more taxes then the law requires, and it is through incorporating that you can take advantage of many of the deductions and advantages that the law provides for.

In this book you will investigate strategies that, when properly implemented, can afford you these basic benefits and much more.

In this book you now have the solutions to many of the problems we face in our search for fulfillment of the American dream. Read about the possibilities, form an action plan, and get started before it's too late—*or just hope you're really lucky!*

1

CHAPTER 1
THE BASICS

1

1

Security In Your Future

■ Real World Corporations and What the Textbooks Say

If you've ever been to a college accounting class you were probably told the reason corporations were formed was to allow people to pool their resources and to provide centralized management of those resources. People who learn about incorporating in college think the reason to incorporate is as simple as a bunch of people getting together, putting their money into a business, and hiring centralized management to run it. In the real world it doesn't quite work that way.

The theory of pooling resources and centralized management really only relates to larger, more sophisticated corporations. Most corporations formed today are small businesses. In fact, many only have one person as the sole shareholder, director, and officer. The main reasons for people to incorporate today are liability protection and tax advantages, which can best be gained through the corporate entity. In this section we will look at the liability protection incorporating can offer. We'll also take a look at why many accountants, and even lawyers, give fatally flawed advice like, "Don't incorporate until you're making at least

1

$50,000 a year." Then we'll look at the myths and misconceptions such advice is founded upon. When you are through with this information, you'll know why it's so important to incorporate. Plus, you'll know how to get protection and savings most people only wish for.

■ Incorporating: The Key to Limited Liability and Personal Protection

As you probably know by now, a corporation is a legal person. As a legal person it is separate from its stockholders, its officers, its directors, and its employees. This means if a corporation is sued, all it can lose is what it has. People who sue the corporation cannot attach the assets of the individual stockholder(s). The corporation limits the liability of the individual persons who are associated with it to the extent of their actual investment in the company.

Let's say you set up a corporation, a legal person and you put $10,000 into the corporation exchange for stock. You now own stock in the corporation and the corporation has $10,000. Now let's say the corporation you formed takes $7,000 and buys a vehicle to use in the corporate business and it takes the rest of the money and hires an employee. You tell your corporate employee to take the corporate vehicle and go run an errand. Your trusty employee goes out with the corporate vehicle and proceeds to run over someone.

1

Now you have a problem because the negligence of that employee will be imputed to the corporation. It almost always is, and yours will probably be no exception. But you incorporated so all you have at risk is the $7,000 car and a couple of thousand dollars in cash. If you were a sole proprietor all your business and personal assets would be on the line.

A wrongful death lawsuit such as the one that would result in our example could easily run into millions of dollars, exceeding insurance policy limits and coverage. A lawsuit like this would ruin most people; incorporation can provide the needed protection. I cannot urge people strongly enough to be prepared. Prepare for the worst, and hope for the best.

There are also lawsuits from employees to consider, such as wrongful termination, discrimination, or sexual harassment. There are customers who could sue for service failures, lost profits, damage to reputation, slander, and more. There are suppliers who could sue, not to mention people who just walk across your yard and slip or step into a hole. The possibilities go on and on.

■ Do These Lawsuits Happen In The Real World?

According to the Public Citizen Group more than

1

19.7 million civil lawsuits were filed in the United States in 2000 alone. According to Jack Farls, President of the National Federation of Independent Businesses, in an article printed in *The Chronicle* of Centralia Washington on May 19, 1995, "The toll of just one lawsuit can be so great that, guilty or innocent, many firms shut their doors, lay off their employees, and vanish into legal graveyards."

Everyone knows about the famous multi-million dollar McDonald's "hot coffee" suit. In the months following that jury award, dozens of similar suits were filed against restaurant owners. Sexual harassment is more and more a danger faced by small businesses. Several years ago, Wal-Mart was on the receiving end of a $50 million sexual harassment verdict from a Jefferson City, Missouri jury.

Still other outrageous lawsuits fill today's newspapers. According to an article in the Harrington, Texas *Valley Morning Star*, from August 7, 1995, a Texas Wal-Mart store was charged with a $5.5 million jury verdict because it allegedly sold .22-caliber bullets to a 19 year-old, who put them into a pistol that was accidentally discharged on a fishing trip.

Even more outrageous is the case involving an Alabama physician who purchased a brand-new black BMW. The physician took the BMW into a body shop to have it "gussied up" and the body shop discovered that the car had been previously painted.

1

Since it had been slightly damaged in shipment, BMW repainted the car. The physician, doing what seems to be all the rage, sued BMW and as a result won $4,000 in compensatory damages and $4 million in punitive damages because his car had been painted twice. Instances of ridiculous and outrageous lawsuits go on and on. The fact of life in the beginning of the new century is that this trend is real, and it could happen to you.

The courts are full of real-life examples of huge lawsuits. If you fire an employee, or just get one upset, you could be facing a lawsuit for wrongful termination and/or intentional infliction of emotional distress, emotional damage, breach of covenant of good faith and fair dealing, and on and on. The lawsuit could not only take business assets but your personal assets as well. Incorporation would limit your liability and protect you.

Our nation's founding fathers would turn over in their graves if they heard about this one. Recently, Pete Van de Punte, a San Antonio, Texas man who owned the Dixie Flag Manufacturing Company, found himself a defendant in a lawsuit in which he wasn't even involved. It seems the alleged victim in the case had stopped to help employees of a business lower a large American flag on a windy day. A gust of wind allegedly whisked the flag and the passer by 70 feet into the air. The flag then ripped and dumped the airborne person to the ground. The resulting lawsuit claimed severe injuries were incurred because the flag was unreasonably dangerous without warning labels, and that the flagpole was defectively designed to

1

allow consumers to become airborne. Pete was sued, even though he neither manufactured nor sold the flag in question. He was sued because he was a manufacturer of flags and happened to be in San Antonio. Like many small business owners innocently dragged into such cases, Van de Punte settled out of court, rather than face the high legal bills and immense waste of time involved in fighting the lawsuit. Unfortunately, many small business owners surrender to out-of-court settlements to protect their businesses from the brutal financial beatings inflicted by today's expensive and lopsided legal system. "Even if an entrepreneur goes to court and wins, his legal fees and court costs could still mean bankruptcy," according to Farls.

Another example is the one about the people who made the mistake of thinking that the English language was sufficient for use in the United States. Several Spanish-speaking farmhands in Texas accidentally killed their boss's prize bull by using pesticide that was lethal to livestock. There was apparently a warning label on the pesticide that told them that the pesticide could kill livestock, but it wasn't in Spanish. The farm workers could not read the label so they used the pesticide and the bull died. Their employer, instead of figuring that it was his own negligence or the negligence of his employees, sued the manufacturer of the pesticide instead. It seems he thought that the warning label should have been in Spanish as well. He was awarded $8.5 million— including $7 million of puntitive damages.

Pretty incredible, an $8.5 million bull! These so-called "nuisance" lawsuits may seem ridiculous, but they are dangerous and can ruin you.

You would think you would actually have to be at fault to be sued and have a court rule against you. We only wish that were the case. As *Forbes* recently put it, "Defendants, particularly if they are perceived to have deep pockets, have begun to find that they run the risk of losing lawsuits, even if their involvement is minimal." Even the most specific contracts to the contrary are ignored. "In a nutshell, the law now says be careless, get paid," summarizes Victor E. Schwartz, a partner with Washington D.C.'s Crowell and Moring. "Not only is it easy to get sued, jury awards and judgments against unsuspecting defendants are going up all the time." *Forbes* stated that, "A rarity just a decade ago, the million dollar plus award is now merely average in San Francisco and Cook County." (*Forbes*, October, 1989).

It's risky out there in the business world.

1

Incorporating doesn't eliminate lawsuits, but it reduces the depth of a person's pocket. Generally, all an incorporated business risks is what's in the corporation.

Why should a business person risk all of his own assets that he has spent a lifetime building up? Why should he risk his family's welfare? There's no good reason, especially when he can do a simple thing like incorporating to limit his exposure. It's such a simple, economical process and yet it's so often overlooked or put off until it's too late.

1

Your Basic Business Structure And Strategy Guide

Many of the strategies used by big business can be used by the small entrepreneur to effect great benefits in tax-planning, asset protection and privacy issues.

You are about to learn how to set up and run your business in a manner that will allow you to take advantage of the laws of our nation, rather than be encumbered by them.

The United States government has no obligation to show anyone how to run their business with the least liability, least tax ramifications and most privacy. It is the citizen's responsibility to learn and properly use strategies that can help them to take advantage of the laws of our nation. Could you imagine a judge presiding over a bankruptcy, or an IRS auditor, both versed in the tax law of our great nation, pulling you aside and telling you, "You know what, just because you are a citizen, we feel you are entitled to know that if you do this, this, or this, you would be eligible for these deductions or rulings in your favor."

You should also be advised that there are many Americans in business who use these strategies but implement the strategies incorrectly, implement them for the wrong reasons, or fail to document the reasons.

1

Whatever the cause, these people may unknowingly be lowering their taxes fraudulently. When the government catches up to them, they are often hit with such a tax liability that it ruins them financially. These people may feel they have protected themselves against the personal liabilities associated with business, only to have their strategies crumble in a court of law.

This is easily avoidable. There are three simple steps that a business must have in place in order to take advantage of any strategy, and they are as follows:

1. You must have a sound and legal business reason behind every decision you make.

2. You must document both the reason behind a decision, and the plan you wish to follow to implement that decision in a timely manner.

3. You must implement that decision according to the letter of the law and fully complete all the steps necessary to give you the right to implement that decision.

What if you could structure your business affairs so that you enjoyed more perks and benefits, a better lifestyle for you and your loved ones and yet, to all appearances, you earned less income, owned less assets, and your business was structured without any personal liability whatsoever?

1

Should your business produce less income due to your ability to enjoy more deductible perks and benefits, then there simply is less income tax! Should your business be structured without personal liability, you have nothing to lose! Should your business have less assets, there is less for that business to lose in a lawsuit!

Privacy is another important issue. Privacy in business will afford you more liability protection. The less someone knows about your assets, the less they will be inclined to sue you. In other words, if you are successful in keeping your private affairs private and everybody thinks you are broke, then nobody will waste money trying to sue you for what they believe you don't have. An attorney researching a case will first try to ascertain whether or not you have assets that can be taken away from you in a lawsuit. If you successfully keep this private information away from the attorney's discovery process, he will turn to his clients and tell them that as far as he knows, you have nothing to sue for. If the clients still wish to pursue the lawsuit, they would have to pay the lawyer on an hourly basis. Most sane people give up at this point.

This is where you come in! Your job is to become well versed with the strategies presented in this book and the opportunities they open up for you.

1

What Is A Corporation?

I wish I had a person whose thoughts I could control, while having him hold title to my assets. Then I could limit my exposure connected with these assets, yet benefit from their use.

A corporation is a legal person, an entity unto itself, with a life and identity all its own. The corporation is not you, and you are not the corporation. A corporation is a person whose thoughts you can control, that can and will defend you against lawsuits, protect all your personal assets and hold title to property.

It's not suprising that roughly a million corporations are formed each year and the number is growing.

A corporation is a distinct legal entity that is separate and apart from its employees, stockholders, directors, and officers. Although it's a separate entity, it can act only through its stockholders, officers, or agents. A stockholder (owner or partial owner) is a holder of shares of stock in the corporation and is not in legal danger. A stockholder is not the employer of those working for the corporation, nor is he the owner of corporate property. His liability is limited entirely to the money he has put into this separate legal person.

1

As an artificial person, a corporation's rights, duties and liabilities do not differ from those of a natural person under similar conditions, except where the exercise of duty would require the ability to comprehend, or think. That's where the Board of Directors comes in. They do the thinking for the corporation. Proof that the directors thought on behalf of the corporation is evidenced by minutes or corporate resolutions. A corporation can buy, trade, sell and make loans—literally anything you as a person can do. These thoughts and actions simply need to be documented by a resolution. When you think it through, the possibilities become fascinating. The key point to remember here is that although you may own a corporation, that corporation exists as a separate entity or person.

You cannot properly deal with or understand any item discussed from this point on until you completely understand this principle. Therefore, if there is anything in this explanation that you do not completely understand, we strongly suggest you keep analyzing it until you do.

1

A Business Entity Analysis

There are various forms of doing business. There are proprietorships, partnerships, LLCs, and corporations. These different business entities and their use can have a great impact on the way you conduct your business, what your personal liability is, and the amount of tax liability you incur.

■ Proprietorships

The advantage of being a sole proprietor is that it is the easiest and simplest form of doing business. As an individual you simply start a business. You are then a sole proprietor. The main disadvantage is the individual proprietor is subject to full liability resulting from his business acts. If the proprietor gets sued because of a related activity, all of his personal assets as well as his business assets are on the line. He could lose everything in a lawsuit.

Sole proprietors are also subject to a 15.3% self-employment tax on all income earned from the business. Furthermore, they do not have available to them benefits such as medical reimbursement plans, certain pension plans, nor full deductibility of business related expenses.

1

■ Partnerships

A partnership is a form of business often used when two or more people get together to conduct a business enterprise. They are simple to form. The partners simply get together and enter into a partnership agreement. From that point on, the gain or loss of the partnership is passed through to the individual partners and is included on their individual tax returns. This creates ease of doing business and simplicity in figuring taxes.

The main disadvantage of a partnership is it provides no liability protection to the partners. If, for example, Joe and Don get together and form a business partnership, and the partnership gets sued and loses, then both Joe's and Don's assets are on the line. Each of them could lose everything. This disadvantage alone is enough to compel those considering a partnership to consider another form of doing business—usually a corporation or a limited liability company.

Another disadvantage is that a partnership doesn't provide many of the tax benefits available to a corporation, such as medical reimbursement plans, pension plans, and full deductibility of business-related expenses. Further, in a partnership, the active partners are subject to a 15.3% self-employment tax on the income they receive from the partnership. This self-employment tax is not an income tax. It is a separate tax that must be paid by certain taxpayers. A corporation is not subject to self-employment tax on its income.

1

■ Limited Partnerships

A limited partnership is taxed like a partnership yet it has many of the liability protection aspects of a corporation. There are two types of partners in a limited partnership: the limited partners, who invest in the partnership but have no control, and the general partner (or partners), who controls the partnership. The problem with the limited partnership is that the general partner has personal liability for certain lawsuits filed by the limited partners against him or in a lawsuit filed against the partnership itself. Therefore, the liability protection that a limited partnership provides is by no means absolute. The general partner is at risk and his personal assets are entirely on the line.

Another drawback to a limited partnership is that it is complex and often expensive to form. Also, as with partnerships and sole proprietorships, the general partner in a limited partnership is subject to the self-employment tax on his or her income. In addition, limited partnerships do not allow for medical reimbursement plans, pension plans, nor the other benefits a corporation offers.

The primary advantage of a limited partnership is it affords the limited partners with limited liability and a single level of taxation. The income that comes into the limited partnership flows through to the partners for tax purposes and is included on their personal tax returns.

1

■ Limited Liability Companies — LLCs

A Limited Liability Company, as its name implies, provides limited liability for its members-owners, like a limited partnership provides for its limited partners or a corporation provides for its shareholders.

Unlike a corporation, LLCs provide members the power of controlling other members' ability to transfer the ownership or voting power of their membership. Like a corporation, an LLC can be structured to be taxed as either a "pass-through" entity or as an association that pays its own taxes.

LLCs have far fewer restrictions on membership than an S-corporation has on shareholders. LLCs also allow members to participate in management of the LLC without losing their protection from liability, whereas a limited partner in a limited partnership does not have this benefit.

The main disadvantage of LLCs is that their use is relatively new in the United States and there is no uniformity in the laws governing LLCs between the individual states. Also, because they are new, there is little case law to help you make decisions based on your state's past decisions concerning LLCs.

1

■ Corporations

The main advantage of incorporating is that it provides limited liability for the owners. If the business is sued, then only the corporation's assets are on the line. If you as a shareholder have only invested $100 in the business, that's all you have at risk. Generally, the shareholders' liability in a corporation is limited to their investment in the corporation, and does not include their personal assets. If the coporation is sued, it's the corporation's problem. Corporations also have great tax advantages and other fringe benefits available to them, such as medical reimbursement plans, pension plans, and full deductibility of business expenses.

The main disadvantage of incorporating is that formation can be complicated. Another disadvantage to the corporate form of business is the so-called "double taxation" problem. Double taxation only occurs when a regular corporation declares a dividend. A regular corporation pays taxes separately from its shareholders and it can't deduct a dividend payment. The shareholders declare the dividend payment as income on their taxes. The income is taxed once at the corporate level and again at the shareholder level, and thus it is taxed twice. Actually, there is no law requiring a corporation to declare a dividend. The corporation can, in fact, retain earnings up to $250,000— even more if the corporation intends to use the money for growth. In most cases since there is no need to declare a dividend, you can avoid the double taxation in a small, closely held corporation. Further, a corporation can elect to be treated

1

as an S-corporation for tax purposes. This means that without first being taxed at the corporate level, all income or losses are passed through to the individual shareholders. Essentially, an S-corporation is treated like a partnership for tax purposes, but it has all the limited liability protection of a regular corporation.

S-corporations, however, don't have many of the fringe benefits that regular corporations do, such as certain pension plans and full deductibility of passive losses against active income. An S-corporation can, however, help you to reduce self-employment taxes while avoiding double taxation.

In summary, a corporation is a legal person, an entity unto itself, with a life and identity all its own. The corporation is not you, and you are not the corporation. A corporation is separate and apart from its employees, stockholders, directors or officers. Although it is a separate entity, it can only act through its officers or agents. A corporation can do anything, except think for itself. The thinking process of a corporation is done by its Board of Directors. Thus, with the Board of Directors to do its thinking, a corporation can do almost anything you as a person can do.

Also, because corporations were the tools solely of big business in America for so long, many perks, benefits and tax loopholes have been made possible for corporations that simply are not available to most other forms of doing business. You as a small corporation owner can now enjoy these same benefits and much more through the implementation of corporate strategies.

CHART I
NON-TAX COMPARISONS OF
DIFFERENT BUSINESS STRUCTURES

Factor	Regular Corporation	S-corporation	Limited Liability Company	Limited Partnership	Partnership
Brief Description	A business entity established by the recording of Articles of Incorporation with the state. It is considered an association that is responsible for paying its own taxes.	A regular corporation that has elected to be treated as a "pass-through" entity that passes its profits and losses through to the shareholders for taxation at a personal level.	A business entity established by the recording of Articles of Organization with the state. It may structure itself to be treated as an association like a regular corporation or as a "pass-through" entity like an S-corporation.	A business entity established by the recording of a partnership agreement with the state. It is always considered a "pass-through" entity.	A business entity established by the agreement between its partners and licensing to do business as a partnership. It is always considered a "pass-through" entity.
Continuity of Life	Unlimited or perpetual unless limited by state law or by its own Articles of Incorporation.	Same as a regular corporation. Election of S-corporation status may be changed without affecting its continuity of life.	Same as a regular corporation. Its election of being treated as an association or "pass through" entity does not affect its continuity of life.	Can be limited to a set period as stated in its agreement, or as long as the partners wish to continue their business relationship. The death, legal disability or withdrawal of a partner will terminate the life.	Can be limited to a set period as stated in its agreement, or as long as the partners wish to continue their business relationship. The death, legal disability or withdrawal of a partner will terminate the life.

1

CHART I
NON-TAX COMPARISONS OF
DIFFERENT BUSINESS STRUCTURES

Factor	Regular Corporation	S-corporation	Limited Liability Company	Limited Partnership	Partnership
Entity Status	A corporation is considered to be completely separate from its owners.	Same as a regular corporation.	Same as a regular corporation.	Same as a regular corporation.	Generally recognized as being separate from its owners, but not for all purposes, such as liability.
Ownership and management structure and the personal liability of the Owners and Managers. (The limited liability that owners enjoy is limited to actions of the business entity not caused by fraudulent actions of the owners.)	Owners are shareholders while management consists of elected or appointed Directors and Officers. While shareholders enjoy limited liability for the actions of the corporation, the Directors and Officers may be indemnified by the corporation for actions of the corporation. (This means the corporation itself can accept liabilities that would otherwise be endured by the Directors and Officers.)	Same as a regular corporation.	Owners are Members while management can be either elected Manager(s) or Manager Members(s). Members enjoy limited liability while managers may be indemnified from actions taken against the LLC by the LLC itself, not unlike the indemnification a corporation can offer its Directors and Officers.	Owners are partners. The General Partner(s) manage the company with full personal liability for the actions of the partnership while Limited Partner(s) have no part in the management of the partnership but enjoy limited personal liability for the actions of the partnership.	Owners and managers are partner(s) in the partnership and share personal liability for the partnership's actions.

1

CHART I
NON-TAX CONSIDERATIONS FOR COMPARISONS OF
DIFFERENT BUSINESS STRUCTURES

Factor	Regular Corporation	S-corporation	Limited Liability Company	Limited Partnership	Partnership
Ease and effect of transfer of ownership interest.	General stock is easily and readily transfer-able along with any voting rights associated with that stock. Transfer of stock has no effect on the corporate entity.	S-corporations are limited as to who is allowed to own the stock and how many stockholders it has in order to maintain its status as an S-corporation and therefore a "pass-through" entity. Transfer is the same as regular corporations, except that the transfer of stock cannot break these limitations if the S-corporation wishes to maintain its "pass-through" status.	All members must approve any transfer of interests by any members. They can allow the transfer of ownership with or without voting rights, or deny the transfer of ownership entirely.	Transfer of ownership in a partnership is overseen by the Partnership Agreement and may require the approval of all partners. The transfer of ownership may require the termination of the old partnership and creation of a new one.	Same as a Limited Partnership.

1

CHART I
NON-TAX CONSIDERATIONS FOR COMPARISONS OF DIFFERENT BUSINESS STRUCTURES

Factor	Regular Corporation	S-corporation	Limited Liability Company	Limited Partnership	Partnership
Availability of outside capital or financing.	May sell stock or bonds to the public. There is no state set limit on the number of shareholders a regular corporation may have, and so it may raise capital through stock issuance. A corporation may also enter into contracts establishing debt so it can borrow money with the corporation itself as the debtor.	Same as regular corporations except that they have a limit on the number of shareholders (75) to whom they can sell stock to raise capital.	Same as regular corporations with no limits on the number of members. However, limitations may be imposed by the members right to deny potential members membership.	Same as regular corporations, but all loans are backed personally by the General Partner(s) and new partners may be limited by the partnership agreement.	All loans to the partnership are backed personally by one or more of the partners and the addition of new partners may be limited by the partnership agreement.

1

CHART II
INCOME TAX CONSIDERATIONS FOR COMPARISONS OF DIFFERENT BUSINESS STRUCTURES

Factor	Regular Corporation	S-corporation	Limited Liability Company	Limited Partnership	Partnership
Who pays the tax?	The corporation is taxed on its taxable income before dividends are paid, whether or not dividends are distributed to the shareholders. The shareholders are taxed personally on any dividends they receive.	The owners are taxed on their share of the profits the business generated, regardless of whether they actually received the cash or it was retained by the business.	Same as a regular corporation if LLC elects to be taxed as an association, and the same as an S-corporation if LLC elects to be taxed as a "pass-through" entity.	The owners are taxed on their share of the profits the business generated, regardless of whether they actually received the cash or it was retained by the business.	The owners are taxed on their share of the profits the business generated, regardless of whether they actually received the cash or it was retained by the business.
Salaries paid to owners.	Where owners are employees, salaries are taxable to the owners and deductible by the corporation. Salaries must remain reasonable for services rendered.	Same as a regular corporation, except that residual profit of the corporation (after salaries and overhead) is passed through as unearned income to the owners.	Same as a regular corporation if LLC elects to be taxed as an association, and the same as an S-corporation if LLC elects to be taxed as a "pass-through" entity.	Same as S-corporation except limited partners may not be employed by the Limited Partnership in any fashion.	Same as S-corporation.
Liquidation of the business.	Amount received by owners in excess of their original investment is usually taxable as capital gain.	Same as a regular corporation.	Same as a regular corporation.	Same as a regular corporation.	Same as a regular corporation.

CHART II

INCOME TAX CONSIDERATIONS FOR COMPARISONS OF DIFFERENT BUSINESS STRUCTURES

Factor	Regular Corporation	S-corporation	Limited Liability Company	Limited Partnership	Partnership
Pension or profit sharing plan.	Owners who are employees can be included in a regular qualified plan.	Same as a regular corporation.	Same as a regular corporation.	Same as a regular corporation, except that limited partners cannot be classified as employees.	Partners may participate only in a qualified self-employment plan.
Capital gains and losses.	Taxed to the corporation; there is no capital gains deduction.	Capital gains and losses normally flow through to the owners as such.	Same as a regular corporation if LLC elects to be taxed as an association, and the same as an S-corporation if LLC elects to be taxed as a "pass-through" entity.	Same as an S-corporation.	Same as an S-corporation.
Can business determine amounts of profits to pay its individual owners regardless of their percentage of ownership?	No.	No.	Yes, if LLC elects to be taxed as a "pass-through" entity and prior agreements have been made by the members and are reasonable.	Yes, if prior agreements have been made by the partners and are reasonable.	Yes, if prior agreements have been made by the partners and are reasonable.

CHART II
INCOME TAX CONSIDERATIONS FOR COMPARISONS OF DIFFERENT BUSINESS STRUCTURES

Factor	Regular Corporation	S-corporation	Limited Liability Company	Limited Partnership	Partnership
Limits and taxation of after-tax earnings accumulated by the business.	May be subject to a penalty tax if amount of accumultation is unreasonable.	No limit since all income is taxed to the owners whether it is distributed or not.	Same as a regular corporation if LLC elects to be taxed as an association, and the same as an S-corporation if LLC elects to be taxed as a "pass-through" entity.	Same as an S-corporation.	Same as an S-corporation.
Passive investment income.	Excessive passive income may cause the regular corporation to be classified as a holding company with a penalty tax imposed on its earnings.	If it has excessive passive income for three consecutive years, the S-corporation may lose its status as a "pass-through" entity and revert to a regular corporation, when it may be classified as a holding company.	Same as a regular corporation if LLC elects to be taxed as an association, and the same as an S-corporation if LLC elects to be taxed as a "pass-through" entity.	No effect.	No effect.
Selection of taxable year ends.	No restriction.	Limited to Dec. 31, or what is commonly referred to as a calendar year. Exceptions are occasionally allowed when calendar year causes undue duress or unwarranted business disadvantage.	Same as a regular corporation if LLC elects to be taxed as an association, and the same as an S-corporation if LLC elects to be taxed as a "pass-through" entity.	Same as an S-corporation.	Same as an S-corporation.

How A Corporation Works

1

■ Who's Who and What They Do

STOCKHOLDERS/OWNERS

Stockholders are the owners of a corporation. As such they are holders of stock certificates. Their primary function related to the corporation is that they elect the Directors. Each share of voting stock is entitled to one vote, which is where control of the corporation comes in.

The Directors carry out the stockholders' wishes and run the corporation in the stockholders' best interests. The end result is to make a profit for the corporation for the benefit of the stockholders.

When a person (or persons) has control of a corporation, they can always call a special meeting and remove directors who are not performing according to their wishes. Also, of no small consequence is the fact that the stockholders may also elect themselves as directors, which is what usually happens in small, privately-held corporations. It always happens in a one-person corporation and is very common and totally acceptable in many states.

1

DIRECTORS

Directors work for the best interests of the stock-holders. The directors are responsible for the general overall management of the corporation. They are the ones who really have the power to "wheel and deal" with the corporation. They set policy to be carried out by the officers and make the major decisions affecting the corporation. They hire the officers, and the officers take orders from them, usually funneled through the president of the corporation. Like the stockholders, the directors make decisions by voting. However, the directors do not have one vote per share of stock—as they are not necessarily stockholders—they have one vote each. For example, if there are three directors, the vote of any two would make a majority or quorum.

OFFICERS

The officers carry out the instructions of the Board of Directors in the matter of day-to-day operations. The officers have the power to run the corporation on a day-to-day basis and make decisions, as long as those decisions are contained within the framework of policy and instruction as handed down by the Board of Directors. The president is in charge of the officers and is the one primarily responsible for reporting to the Board of Direc-

1

tors. The responsibilities of both the directors and officers are usually spelled out in the bylaws of the corporation as set down by the stockholders and/or directors.

The officers of the corporation also have considerable legal responsibility. They are, for example, responsible for seeing that the payroll taxes withheld by the corporation are paid to the I.R.S. In the event that they fail to perform that responsibility, they are held personally liable and responsible for those payments.

EMPLOYEES

Employees are hired by the officers to carry out their instructions and perform duties consistent with those instructions on a day-to-day basis.

1

Running a Corporation By The Book

■ If It Looks Like A Duck And Acts Like A Duck, It Must Be A Duck

You can be a stockholder, a director, an officer and an employee of the same corporation. The difficult part of a one-person corporation is that you must remember at all times which function you are serving in. When choosing yourself as director for the corporation, you are acting as a stockholder. When drafting corporate resolutions, you're acting as a secretary. When signing contracts or other documents, you're acting as an officer. When sweeping the floor you are acting in the capacity of an employee. In one-person corporations such as this, corporate formalities become the crucial element of proof that you are in fact doing business as a corporation, rather than as a sole proprietor. "Corporate formalities" is a

1

term which encompasses certain functions within the operation of a corporation which prove that a corporation is acting properly. Corporate formalities include annual meetings of stockholders and directors, minutes of meetings, Board of Directors resolutions (which document the directors' thinking), and proper appointment of officers. Small, one-person corporations have the greatest difficulty with corporate formalities. They experience difficulty, not because corporate formalities are difficult, but rather because many business people forget to observe them. The best way to avoid problems is simply to keep up with your corporate records, hold your annual meetings, and stop and think which role you are playing at any given time. Entrepreneurs who do so seldom find this to be difficult or onerous.

■ More on Corporate Formalities

Now let's talk about the most important thing regarding the operation of your corporation. What are corporate formalities? They are, simply stated, the responsibilities of keeping your corporate records in compliance with all laws and regulations.

You've probably heard about lawyers piercing the corporate veil—going around the corporation to hold the owners personally liable for its debts. This is tragic, especially since it's so easy to prevent.

In order for a corporation to be treated as a corporation, it must look and act like a corporation. Just like the old saying, "If it looks like a duck, walks

1

like a duck, and quacks like a duck, it's a duck."
Well, if a corporation looks like a corporation and
acts like a corporation, it's a corporation. If not,
it's not a corporation, and the courts won't treat it
like one.

How do you make sure a corporation looks and
acts like a corporation? Well, the first thing is to
make sure all of your letterheads, stationery, business cards, statements, etc.—anything you write
or say about your business—should say "Inc.,"
"Corp," "Co.," or "Ltd." Then your business looks
like a corporation and you are presenting it to the
public as being a corporation.

Furthermore, when you set up a corporation, you
should give it a reasonable amount of money to carry
out its purpose. You can do that by buying stock in
your corporation. This need not be a lot of money;
in fact, in most cases a few thousand dollars is sufficient.

As previously noted, a corporation can do everything
you can do, except think. The corporation's thinking is done for it by the Board of Directors. Therefore, when the corporation has thought, those
thoughts must be reduced to written form and contained in the corporate records as proof that it was,
in fact, the corporation that thought and acted. Each
time a corporation makes any major decision, it
should be noted in the corporate record book in the
form of minutes or resolutions.

1

When that is done, the corporate entity is preserved and safe.

In fact, the fewer stockholders a corporation has, the more important this becomes. Certainly in the case of a one-person corporation, it is literally all important!

You will often hear stories of outsiders "penetrating the corporate veil." We submit that this seldom happens and that a corporation cannot be penetrated if the corporate formalities are properly followed—assuming there is no fraud or wrongful intent. That is why it is all important to observe corporate formalities. Courts look at the corporate records to determine if the corporation acted as a corporation or as an individual. If it acted as a corporation, all decisions are documented as proof that it was the corporation acting, not the individual. Therefore, if the corporation documents its acts by minutes or resolutions, then the individual is insulated from the acts of the corporation.

You may have heard of the Alter Ego theory. That is where outsiders attempt to prove that the corporation is not a corporation but simply another instrument or charade of an individual. Whether or not this allegation will stand up depends on whether or not the corporate formalities have been properly observed.

The bottom line is, to be treated and recognized as a corporation, you must look and act like a corporation and observe the corporate formalities which are as follows:

1

a. **Required Meeting:** Annual meetings are not always required of the stockholders and directors, but these meetings help to document the actions of the corporation as well as provide proof of the ongoing pursuit of the purpose for the corporation to exist. Therefore, they should be properly recorded in the corporation record book.

b. **Minutes Of Meetings:** When a meeting is held for any purpose, it is important to observe the corporate formalities and document said meeting in the corporate record book.

c. **Resolutions:** Aside from the required annual meetings, the easiest way to govern and observe corporate formalities in a small, private corporation is by resolutions signed by a quorum of its directors or stockholders (as applicable). Put many resolutions in your corporate record book concerning everything you do, and you will be protecting both the corporation and the individual stockholders.

d. **Articles/Bylaws:** The corporation must comply with the rules and regulations set forth by the corporation in these documents. Study them closely, comply with them, and again, you will be observing corporate formalities. Nothing about a corporation is irrevocable. If you as a majority do not like either of those documents at any time, or you think they should be changed, it's very simple—change them!

1

e. **Corporate Seal:** In most states, the corporate seal is required on official documents of the corporation. Though it is not required in a few states, many people think it is, so it's important no matter where your corpoation is domiciled.

f. Never commingle your personal funds or expenditures with those of the corporation. The corporation must have its own checking account for business purposes only. Do not pay personal expenses out of the corporate checking account. For instance, do not write a corporate check for groceries. Do not write a corporate check for cash, without an explanation as to where the cash went. Keep your accounts clean. Also, for tax reasons, it is vital to put adequate explanations on the corporate checks you write and to have receipts or cash tickets to back them up. For example, in the case of a company car, the corporation pays all the expenses, and the checks must be made out so this is readily ascertainable. You, as an individual, may be reimbursed by the corporation for cash tickets for gasoline, oil changes and so on. So, when the corporation writes you a check for those items, the check should be identified as "Reimbursement for cash tickets attached", and they should be listed. This procedure keeps personal and business monies separate and helps to keep your accounts clean and your records straight.

1

g. Another important corporate formality is proper signatures. When you sign anything on behalf of the corporation, such as invoices, delivery receipts, contracts or other items of indebtedness, always sign everything "XYZ Corporation, by John Doe, President" (or Secretary, or Treasurer, or whatever your capacity is). This gives public notice you are signing as an officer of the corporation and not as an individual. This is one of the formalities that prevents piercing of the corporate veil.

If you sign as an individual, anyone can say they thought that's what you obviously intended, because that is what you wrote. By signing as an individual, you are standing alone.

In order to be treated like a corporation, your corporation must look and act like one. If you don't treat it like a corporation, no one else will. It's so easy to do, just several pieces of paper per year and it's so important.

When You Should Incorporate

1

■ **Myth: "Don't incorporate until you've reached a certain point in your business, like making $50,000 per year."**

Advice such as that totally ignores the possibility that a person could be sued. It only takes taxes into consideration and taxes pale in comparison to the possibility of losing everything. One should consider both taxes and liability when thinking of incorporating. The sad part about all of this is such advice isn't even good tax advice. It's true that you have to earn some revenue before you can reap all of the tax benefits of incorporating but it's only fair to mention that there are tax benefits from losing money with the corporation too. When you look at the tax benefits available to you through incorporating, even if you never make a profit, you will see that advice such as the above is actually a disservice to the one receiving it. This is especially true when you consider both taxes and the urgent need for liability protection.

If you're in business or going into business, the time to incorporate is now. Actually, yesterday would not have been too soon. If you get sued tomorrow, the amount of money you would have spent to incorporate will seem like peanuts.

1

Further, you really don't lose tax benefits by in-corporating. Any advice to the contrary is simply based on a lack of understanding and a failure to consider all the facts.

When someone says don't incorporate now, they are generally coming from one of the following positions:

First, if you incorporate and lose money, you lose your personal tax loss deduction on your personal return. The corporation would have the tax loss, not you.

Second, you shouldn't spend the money on incorporating until you are sure you are going to succeed. If you don't succeed, you won't benefit from lower corporate tax brackets, pension and medical reimbursement plans, and passive loss deductions available to corporations. Consider, however, these points:

In the first situation, if you are worried about taking personal tax deductions for your business losses, consider that the law allows you to create what is commonly called an S-corporation. The S-corporation will pass through the losses to you and you can take advantage of personal tax losses.

Further, even if you don't elect "S" status for your corporation and your business becomes worthless, Section 1244 of the Internal Revenue Code allows you to write off those losses on your personal tax return. That's up to $50,000 if you're single and up to $100,000 if you're married and filing a joint return.

1

You simply do not lose personal tax loss benefits if you do things right.

Now let's consider the second position, which is that you don't benefit from corporate perks and lower tax rates up to certain income levels if you're not making money. That may be true but you can benefit from the losses now and the lower rates later. Not only can you get the personal benefits from losses like we've talked about above, but a regular corporation, as contrasted to an S-corporation, can carry forward its losses for 15 years. That's right, if a corporation loses money this year and goes into the hole, for say $20,000, then it has a $20,000 loss going into next year. If it makes $20,000 next year it pays no tax.

So, even if the corporation loses money, there are tax benefits and this translates into benefits for you. Even if you did not take advantage personally under subchapter S of the corporation's losses while it was losing money, you still get to write off the value of the money you put into the business by claiming a stock loss under Section 1244. Thus, you still get personal tax benefits from corporate losses. In addition, while trying to make money with the business, you've been doing it with the personal protection of a corporation and your personal assets have not been put in jeopardy.

1

Those who tell you that you must make at least $50,000 a year are telling you that you'll probably fail. They're telling you that because 90% of new businesses do fail within the first five years. They are presuming you'll fail too. They're saying your corporation is going to lose money and you'll not gain any benefit from the loss. That's just not true if you do things right. It's like what the successful salesperson said when asked, "Why are you so successful?" The successful salesperson simply replied, "It's all in knowing how." So, when should you incorporate? NOW!—for liability protection as well as probable tax advantages.

■ The $50K Myth

1

The following table shows how a family business that nets as little as $30,000 a year can conceivably lower their taxes by as much as 50% through using an S-corporation versus a sole proprietorship.

	Family Business 1 (Proprietorship)	Family Business 2 (S-corporation)
Wages	$ 0	$12,000
Schedule C	40,000	0
Schedule E (from Form 1120S K-1)	0	40,000
Less: Personal Salary		(12,000)
Child No. 1		(4,250)
Child No. 2		(4,250)
Corporate Payroll Taxes		(1,662)
Adjusted Gross Income	40,000	29,838
Less 50% Self Employment Tax	(2,826)	
Less: Itemized	(10,000)	(10,000)
Exemptions (4 x $2,700)	(10,800)	(10,800)
Taxable Income	16,374	9,038
Income Tax	2,456	1,355
Self Employment Tax	5,652	
Corporate Payroll Taxes		1,662
W-2 - S.S./Medicare Tax Withheld		918
	———	———
TOTAL TAXES	$ 8,108	$ 3,935

This is a savings of over 50%. Now let somebody tell you that incorporating is not a good idea for businesses earning less than $50,000 per year.

1

What Is An S-Corporation?

An S-corporation is a regular corporation whose stockholders elect to qualify it under Section 1361 to Section 1379 of the Internal Revenue Code. A common misconception is that there is something special, peculiar or extra to be done in forming an S-corporation. That is not true. An S-corporation is a regular corporation, just like any other corporation at the outset. The newly formed corporation may remain a regular C-corporation or you, the stockholder(s), may convert it to an S-corporation under the IRS Code.

Some rules do exist for corporations that wish to obtain S-corporation status. There can be no more than 75 shareholders. There can only be one class of stock. Shareholders can only be U.S. citizens, resident aliens, estates, certain trusts, or certain qualified tax exempt organizations. There are a few more criteria that a corporation must meet to gain the S-corporation status but most small, closely-held corporations will have no problem doing so. Please seek professional advice should you have more questions about the formation of S-corporations.

1

Those who have not worked with S-corporations often believe there is some horrendous procedure to go through or some mysterious red tape that must be dealt with in order to qualify as an S-corporation. Not true! To elect S-corporation status with the federal government, you simply fill out a one-page form, front and back, and mail it to the IRS. That's it. In states that require income tax, such as California, it may be necessary for the corporation to file a form with the state in order to be treated as an S-corporation for state income tax purposes.

An S-corporation is one that generally pays no income tax. It is exempt from paying income tax by virtue of its S-corporation election. Instead of the corporation paying tax, the profit or loss of the corporation flows through to the individual stockholders' personal tax returns in the *pro rata* amount of their stock ownership in the corporation. The corporation simply files an 1120-S and issues K-1s to the stockholders.

An S-corporation election does have to be filed according to certain time limitations. If your corporation is newly formed, you should file Form 2553 within 75 days of your date of incorporation unless you have done absolutely nothing with your corporation, in which case you can wait longer than 75 days.

1

In other words, if you have purchased a newly-formed corporation shell, you have 75 days from the date that you issue the stock to the shareholders, commence doing business, or the corporation acquires assets. Prior to that time, you cannot have done any business as a corporation. You cannot have transferred any assets to your corporation. If you even so much as open a corporate bank account with $10, this avenue is not available to you. Note that this does not mean that your corporation cannot elect S-corporation status. It simply means that your corporation cannot elect S-corporation status for the current tax year. It can elect S-corporation status for the next tax year but if you have an existing corporation, as opposed to a new one, you can elect S-corporation status within 75 days after the beginning of any given corporate tax year.

1

The Limiting Qualifications Of An S-Corporation

■ With an S-corporation, revenue and expenses flow through to the shareholders in nearly the same fashion as revenue and expenses of a partnership flows through to its partners.

■ S-corporations are limited to no more than 75 shareholders.

■ Shareholders of S-corporations can only be U.S. citizens, resident aliens, estates, certain trusts, or certain qualified tax-exempt organizations.

■ S-corporations can only have one class of stock. (Note: Warrants, options or certain debt instruments might be deemed as a class of stock and cause the loss of S treatment.)

■ Members of an affiliated group are ineligible to become S-corporations.

■ An S-corporation can own a C-corporation but an S-corporation may not have a C-corporation stockholder.

1

■ S-corporations must make and file an election with the IRS to be an S-corporation.

■ An S-corporation's election is terminated whenever the corporation has excessive passive income from prior C-corporation earnings for three consecutive years.

Should any of these limitations appear to be a problem for your business structure, you should investigate using a limited liability company (LLC) instead of an S-corporation. In fact, it may be a good idea to use an LLC rather than an S-corporation if you will be using it to hold investments or property. See Section III for more information on LLCs.

Money In Your Pocket

Now that we've seen what a corporation is and how it stacks up against other forms of doing business, a natural question to ask would be who should incorporate. To decide whether or not incorporating is for you, you need to ask yourself a few questions. First, you should ask, "What is my liability picture?" Second, you should ask, "Do I have assets that I wish to protect?" Third, ask yourself, "Will incorporating benefit me from a tax perspective?"

Anyone in a business or profession who interacts with people, clients, or other businesses should be incorporated. If a business deal goes sour or if a mistake is made in handling a customer's request, the first reaction in today's world is to sue.

1

Even nuisance lawsuits are dangerous. For example, Forbes magazine published an article in October of 1986 which details the following story.

Ernest Canon, attorney, won $23 million for a five-year-old client who was severely injured while riding a lawn mower. Canon convinced the jury that the manufacturer, Ariens Company, was grossly negligent. Punitive damages in the case were $13 million! As though this child's parents should have let a five-year-old ride a lawn mower to begin with! At first glance, you'd think, "What a ridiculous lawsuit!" The fact is that it was worth $23 million.

Of course, anyone in a potentially hazardous business, such as contracting, excavating, heavy equipment operation or the like should incorporate. The potential to claim personal harm on the part of people working for the company or bystanders looking for a quick buck is huge in these types of businesses.

People who are involved in joint ventures or partnerships should also consider incorporation. If you are in a partnership with a person and that person does something to get the partnership sued, your personal assets as well as theirs are on the line. By contrast, if the business were a corporation instead of a partnership, only the corporation's assets would be at risk.

From a liability protection standpoint, there is something else to consider as well. It's hard to believe that just owning something can get a person sued but it can.

1

Take the case of a person who owned several pieces of real estate on which there was a light pole. An individual was sleeping by the pole when a truck came by and hit the pole. The pole fell on the person sleeping under it. The truck had no insurance and the person driving it wasn't worth very much. On the other hand, the property owner was worth quite a bit. The injured individual sued the property owner for failure to secure the pole properly. The injured party took the position that the owner of the property should have made sure the pole was so secure that a truck could not knock it down. Yes, it's a ridiculous lawsuit but it shows just how easy it is to get sued. Simply owning an asset can create liability. Therefore, people who own assets which could be associated with liability should incorporate. This would limit their liability and potential lawsuits to those assets.

What's the bottom line? It is probably easier to outline who should not incorporate than who should. The people who should not incorporate are simply those who don't have a business and are not going into business. They are people who have no assets and have no plan or desire to accumulate assets. Anyone in business, going into business, anyone with valuable assets or working to acquire valuable assets should consider incorporating.

Aside from the liability protection incorporating affords, it can also provide many tax benefits for those thinking of starting a business. For example, a couple selling their own paintings on the side in addition

1

to their primary employment may not conceive of any liability problem. However, by using a corporation properly, they may see enormous tax savings, which could more than justify incorporating.

When all is said and done, incorporating is beneficial to most people in the area of liability protection, as well as tax savings. The next two sections of this book will outline how and why corporations should be used in both these areas.

Many business people have received well-meaning but inadequate advice from tax professionals who tell them not to incorporate unless they're making $50,000 per year. Such advice might have merit from a tax standpoint; but from a liability standpoint, it is often catastrophic. As anyone in business can tell you, you can be sued just as easily making $20,000 a year as you can making $100,000 a year. Advice such as that mentioned above has resulted in hundreds of thousands of bankruptcies across America when people earning under a certain magic number have become victims of a lawsuit.

The simple fact is any person now engaging in business needs to be incorporated. This advice is heard more and more frequently in today's environment. Experts, such as the well-known radio business advisor Bruce Williams, say over and over that they would never engage in business today without being incorporated.

1

When we find highly respected individuals such as Mr. Williams giving this advice, we should realize that this is not something to be taken lightly.

Anyone who is involved in a business where there are employees should be incorporated. Lawsuits against a business for the negligent acts of its employees are widespread.

As if that weren't bad enough, lawsuits from employees are also very common today. Suits regarding wrongful termination and sexual harassment are more and more frequent and judgment awards for such suits are going higher and higher. Steven A. Bokat, Vice President and General Counsel of the U.S. Chamber of Commerce says, "Work place litigation is causing unbelievable problems for employers. You fully expect that every time you discharge an employee, don't promote an employee, or demote an employee, you're going to get a lawsuit. That was not true even 10 years ago." This quote was taken from *Nation's Business*, July 1989. Since then, the situation has grown worse.

1

Gain Ultimate Protection By Using Two Corporations

If one corporation is good, are two corporations better? Many times, yes! As the litigation explosion heats up, many business people are finding that with two corporations they can separate their risks and minimize their lawsuit exposure. Let's say you have two business locations. Put them into separate corporations and run each as a separate entity. This has the desirable effect of limiting the potential for loss to one location.

Other business people go even further. When they set up two corporations. The first corporation conducts business, and the second corporation leases a great deal of its assets to the first corporation. The chances of the second corporation being sued are slim because its main customer is the first corporation which you still own. If the second corporation is sued, while there are some assets at risk, the bulk of the assets are owned by the first corporation which is not subject to the lawsuit.

Another possibility is putting different assets into different corporations to spread out the risk. For example, let's say you own multiple apartment

1

buildings. By putting each apartment building into a separate corporation, if a tenant living in one apartment building sues, that suit is brought against only the corporation that owns the one apartment building. Only one apartment building is at risk and the others are secure. All things considered, this is a very inexpensive way of protecting your assets.

Corporations provide many exciting opportunities for asset protection. When you consider the power available to you in being able to create legal people at will, the benefits are numerous. You've probably heard the old saying, "Don't put all your eggs in one basket." Well, we might say, "Don't put all your assets into one corporation." By limiting the amount of assets in each corporation, you limit your exposure to liability, an enormous benefit if you are hit with a lawsuit.

CHAPTER 2
YOUR CORPORATE STRATEGY

2

CHAPTER TWO
Lower Your Risk Of
A Tax Audit

2

■ High Risk or Low Risk—It's Your Decision

Once there were two fellows, Jack and Roger. They were sitting in their den having a conversation in front of the window when a squad of police cars pulled up outside the house.

Jack opened the window to see what was happening. Hordes of officers jumped out of their cars and started shooting bullets through the window. Jack quickly hit the floor while Roger merely sat there with his arms crossed, gazing through the window. "Get down!" Jack cried. "Why?" Roger responded, "I don't have to protect myself, I didn't do anything wrong."

This sounds pretty ridiculous but many taxpayers are unknowingly acting the same as Roger. Just because you get audited, doesn't mean you're at fault but who wants to spend the time and money on an audit? Even though you are an honest taxpayer, there is no reason for you to stay in a position where you are likely to get hit by an audit.

2

The following, taken from the July, 1986 issue of *Tax Hotline*, should be of great interest to you and hopefully aid you in some of your business planning.

HOT: Lower audit risk. Incorporating your business lowers the chance of an IRS audit. Reason: Only 1.12% of incorporated businesses that filled in Form 1120 with less than $100,000 income were audited as compared to 2.65% of unincorporated businesses with incomes of $25,000 to $100,000 that were audited in the same year. It's worse for the unincorporated businesses as income gets higher. Five percent of unincorporated businesses with income over $100,000 were audited. Incorporated audits for the same income barely rose from the 1.12% figure.

Don't just sit there in front of the window—get out of the line of fire! Even an audit that comes out in your favor can cost you money and time.

Tax Benefits That
Benefit Your Bottom Line

2

■ More On Tax Benefits Of Family Employment

Honey, I employed the kids! Are you married with children? By incorporating a family business and employing family members, taxpayers can reduce their taxes, while building an investment vehicle for their children.

The following two tables show the difference in tax consequences for a family with two children, under the ages of 18, running a small business as a proprietorship versus a corporation.

Both businesses earn $150,000 and net $75,000 after expenses but before federal taxes. Both examples have $10,000 in itemized deductions. Table 1 shows that there are no tax consequences for the employed children, who each receive $6,250 a year, $2,000 of which is placed in an IRA.

	Table 1 EACH CHILD'S 1040 FORM	
	Family Business 1 (Proprietorship)	Family Business 2 (Corporation)
Wages	$0	$6,250
IRA	0	2,000
Standard Deduction	0	4,250
TAXABLE INCOME	0	0

2

Table 2 compares the proprietorship to the corporation. As president of the corporation, the father pays himself a salary of $18,000 a year. (We have assumed that the corporation is an S-corporation).

2

Table 2 PARENTS' 1040 FORM		
	Family Business 1 (Proprietorship)	Family Business 2 (Corporation)
Wages	$0	$18,000
Schedule C	75,000	0
Schedule E (from Form 1120S K-1)	0	75,000
Less: Personal Salary		(18,000)
Child No. 1		(6,250)
Child No. 2		(6,250)
Corporate Payroll Taxes		(2,493)
Adjusted Gross Income	75,000	60,007
Less: 50% Self-Employment Tax	(5,246)	
Less: Itemized	(10,000)	(10,000)
Exemptions (4 x $2,700)	(10,800)	(10,800)
Taxable Income	(48,954)	(39,207)
Income Tax	8,208	5,884
Self-Employment Tax	10,491	
Corporate Payroll Taxes		2,493
W-2 - S.S./Medicare Tax Withheld		1,377
TOTAL TAXES	$18,699	$9,754

A quick glance at the bottom line shows that the incorporated family business ends up with a tax bill $8,945 less than the proprietorship. In addition, the parents will see their children's IRAs grow untaxed. The children's salaries would be used to pay for their general expenses with pre-tax dollar expenses that otherwise would come out of their parent's after-tax income.

By redistributing the money in a corporation, you can legally cut the taxes you owe. This simple illustration shows the power of what is called "income-splitting."

The 1993 Tax Reconciliation Act

2

■ The Small Corporations and You

The 1993 Revenue Reconciliation Act (the Clinton Tax Plan) has been widely regarded as a tax increase. While the top individual rate was increased to 39.6% and the top corporate rate was increased to 35%, that doesn't necessarily have to mean a tax increase for you. Through the proper use of corporations, you can enjoy lower taxes and a sense of security from knowing that your tax planning moves are legal and aboveboard.

Let's take a look at exactly what the Clinton Tax Plan did to individuals and corporations with regard to the new tax rates.

INDIVIDUAL TAX RATES FOR 1998

MARRIED FILING JOINTLY

$0 to $42,350	15% of taxable income
$42,351 to $102,300	$6,352 plus 28% on excess over $42,350
$102,301 to $155,950	$23,138 plus 31% on excess over $102,300
$155,951 to $278,450	$39,770 plus 36% on excess over $155,950
$278,451 and above	$83,870 plus 39.6% on excess over $278,450

SINGLE TAXPAYER

$0 to $25,350	15% of taxable income
$25,351 to $61,400	$3,802.50 plus 28% on excess over $25,350
$61,401 to $128,100	$13,896.50 plus 31% on excess over $61,400
$128,101 to $278,450	$34,573.50 plus 36% on excess over $128,100
$278,451 and above	$88,699.50 plus 39.6% on excess over $278,450

2

As you can see, single individuals with incomes over $128,100 and married couples filing a joint return with incomes over $155,950, will pay substantially more in taxes because a 36% tax rate applies to those groups. The picture doesn't get any prettier for singles or married people filing a joint return who earn over $278,450 per year. Income amounts over $278,450 a year for singles and married couples are taxed at a new 39.6% tax rate. Prior to the Clinton Tax Plan, the highest tax rate an individual would be hit with was 31%. Now it's over 40% due to the phase out of deductions in high income brackets.

Obviously, single individuals with incomes over $128,100 and married couples with incomes over $155,950 will need to take a hard look at their taxes and make some planning moves. These are the people who will be hit the hardest by the Clinton Tax Plan.

If this is you, you need to do something.

Individuals and couples earning less than $128,100 or $155,950, respectively, can also take steps to cut their tax liability.

2

■ Corporate Tax Rates for 2001

The table on page 68 shows you that the 15% bracket, the lowest tax bracket for both corporations and individuals, is much more beneficial for a corporation than an individual or married couple filing jointly. The amount of income that the lowest rate applies is $7,650 greater than it would be for a married couple filing a joint return and $24,650 greater for a single person. The corporation gets from $8,800 to $23,350 more income taxed at the lowest possible rate. In addition to that, a corporation pays only 25% for income levels between $50,000 and $75,000, whereas a married couple filing a joint return would pay 28% and a single person would pay 31% on most income over $61,400. In other words, compared to being married filing a joint return or single, a corporation comes out better because it gets more of its income taxed at the lower 15% and 25% rates. The first $75,000 of net income to a corporation is taxed at a lower rate than if that same $75,000 were taxed to you as an individual, regardless of whether you are married filing a joint return or single.

When you reach $75,000 or greater, of net income the corporate tax rate is 34%. For a married couple filing a joint return, incomes between $75,000 and $102,300 are taxed at 28%. The excess over that is taxed at 31% until that couple's income reaches $155,950. It is then taxed at 36% up to $278,450 when the surtax rate of 39.6% applies.

2

A single person finds a 31% tax bracket on income between $61,400 to $128,100. At $128,100, the 36% rate kicks in until income reaches a level of $278,450. Then the 39.6% surtax kicks in. What's it all mean?

For a single person, it means that a corporation with up to $173,583 in net taxable income will pay less tax. For a married couple filing a joint return, it means that by incorporating you'll save money on a net income of up to $102,223.

Quick Reference Charts

2

Proprietorship vs. Corporation Tax Demonstrates Self-Employment Tax Impact

Taxable Income in $	Amount of S.E. Tax Included	Proprietor Effective Rate & Marginal Tax	Proprietor Tax Total	Corporate Tax Total
Rate 0-25,000	$3,825	$3,750	$7,575	$3,750
Rate 25,001-50,000	$3,825	$6,733.50	$18,133.50	$7,500
Rate 50,001-75,000	$3,825	$7,283.50	$29,242	$13,750
Rate 75,001-100,000	$1,394	$7,750	$38,386.60	$22,250
Rate 100,001-125,000	$725	$7,750	$46,861.60	$32,000
Rate 125,001-150,000	$725	$8,412.50	$55,999.10	$41,750
Rate 150,001-200,000	$1,450	$18,000	$75,449.10	$61,250

Individual vs. Corporate Tax

Taxable Income in $	Married Filing Jointly Marginal Amount Of Tax	Corporate Marginal Amount Of Tax	Married Filing Jointly Total Amount Of Tax	Corporate Total Amount Of Tax
Applicable Rate → 0-25,000	15% $3,750	15% $3,750	$3,750	$3,750
Applicable Rate 50,000	28% $6,733.50	15% $3,750	$10,483.50	$7,500
Applicable Rate → 75,000	31% $7,000	25% $6,250	$17,767	$13,750
Applicable Rate 100,000	31% $7,000	34% $8,500	$25,517	$22,250
Applicable Rate → 125,000	31% $713	39% $9,750	$33,267	$32,000
Applicable Rate 150,000	31% $16,632	39% $9,750	$41,379.50	$41,750
Applicable Rate → 200,000	36% $44,100	39% $19,500	$59,679.50	$61,250
Applicable Rate 250,000	39.6% $22,394	39% $19,500	$77,679.50	$80,750
Applicable Rate → 300,000	39.6% $3,827,340	39% $19,500	$95,776.70	$100,250
Applicable Rate 400,000	39.6% $1,980,000	35% $35,750	$135,376.70	$136,000
Applicable Rate → 500,000	39.6% $1,320,000	34% $34,000	$174,976.70	$170,000
Applicable Rate 1,000,000	39.6% $660,000	34% $170,000	$174,976.70	$340,000

2

How To Save 41.7% Or More In Taxes

2

Senator Bradley said, on the floor of the Senate while debating passage of a tax bill, "I am afraid if we pass this bill, taxpayers will go to their lawyers and accountants and they will show them how to spread income."

Spreading income, or income splitting, is an old strategy that has been used ever since the income tax was first instituted. It is a simple strategy that becomes more attractive under current tax laws.

Let's say, for example, that you are married and file a joint return.

Taxation in our country is a graduated system based upon your "net taxable income." The more you earn, the higher the percentage of taxation you must bear. In other words, as you earn more income, the higher the tax bracket you are taxed in.

Income splitting is possible because you can create a separate taxpayer by forming a corporation. If your corporation were to pay you for services you render, you effectively split the total income realized from your business endeavors. Of course, your goal in splitting income is to position yourself and your corporation in the lowest possible tax bracket.

The tax brackets for you as an individual are different from those of a corporation. The most you can make as a married couple filing jointly and still remain in the lowest possible tax bracket of 15% is $42,350. The most a corporation can earn and still remain in the lowest possible tax bracket of 15% is $50,000.

If you earned a taxable net income of $92,350 in 1998, this would cause you to owe $23,407.50 in federal taxes. That's an overall tax percentage of 25.35%

If, instead, you earned the same $92,350 as a corporation and pay yourself $42,350 for services, this leaves $50,000 in the corporation to be taxed at only 15% creating a tax of $7,500. The $42,350 that you are paid by the corporation is also taxed at only 15% creating a tax of $6,352.50, which equal a $11,505 savings when you combine the two. Now you may not wish to leave this much in your corporation but this example does show you the true power of spreading or splitting income between multiple entities.

Additionaly, corporations have more perks and deductions under the Federal Tax Code than individuals. When you incorporate, your corporation can do things like pay 100% of your medical insurance premiums, as well as 100% of your medical expenses within the framework of a medical reimbursement plan; set up a pension plan for your

2

retirement and deduct the money contributed to it, while you continue to control and invest the money and do it all tax free until you retire!

It is also note worthy that a corporation does not pay the self-employment tax of 15.3% on its income as does an individual. In addition, unlike an individual, the corporation is not subject to the 2% to 3% of adjusted gross income exclusion for itemized deductions or the 7.5% of adjusted gross income exclusion for medical expenses. The corporation gets to deduct 100% of these things right from the start.

Because a corporation enjoys more deductible expenses that you can pay for with pre-tax dollars, it will take a corporation a lot more gross income to reach a given net income. In other words, the corporation can earn a lot more money than you can as an individual and still have a lower taxable net income.

■ What Happens With Two Corporations?

2

Let's say you have an S-corporation and hire your children just as you did in the previous section but you also have a marketing company that is a C-corporation. This time, however, your S-corporation grosses $175,000 and it pays the marketing corporation $110,000 for its services. This leaves you with $65,000 gross income on your schedule E for your S-corporation, instead of $75,000 as in the previous example. Then pay yourself $8,000 instead of the $18,000 as we did in the prior example. Your marketing corporation pays you a $10,000 salary for your services, which brings your salary back up to $18,000.

So far it's all a wash except the marketing corporation (C-corporation) now has $100,000 in income to pay taxes on. Or does it? Let's say the marketing corporation, like the S-corporation, has normal expenses of $10,000 for office space, utilities, phone, etc. That leaves $90,000 in gross income. To help you earn this extra $100,000, you hire an assistant who does anything you need done for $25,000 in salary. Gross income is now down to $65,000.

After purchasing a company car for $28,000 cash, you're down to $37,000.

2

You place $5,000 (half the amount of your salary) into a non-qualified investment pension plan which is a write-off for the corporation and grows tax-free. This leaves $32,000.

You go one step further and also form a non-qualified pension plan with your S-corporation. Investing half of your $8,000 salary from that corporation and paying the C-corporation $4,000 less for its services, now leaves $28,000.

To ensure that you'll never be out of touch with your office, you invest $5,000 in a state-of-the-art home computer networked to your business computer. This leaves $23,000. Being prudent, you place $5,000 in your Medical Reimbursement Plan. (It's good for whatever the doctor orders!) This leaves $18,000. There is business growth to think about, so you invest $9,000 in a system that will double your business over the next few years. (This could be equipment or a new marketing plan.) This leaves $9,000.

With three trips to Disneyland, Disneyworld, and that second honeymoon to Hawaii (I mean those business trips to Los Angeles, Orlando, and Honolulu) which cost $6,000, you are left with $3,000. You also spent $3,000 on those creative retreats/seminars/workshops in Lake Tahoe and Aspen last winter.

You're thinking you're broke and have no tax liabilities, until you remember you received $4,000 in dividends from stocks you invested in with the C-corporation (smart, the corporation only pays taxes on 30% of these dividends)! That means the marketing company you formed as a regular C-corporation must pay $180 in taxes (30% of $4,000 is $1,200, 15% tax on $1,200 is $180).

You decide to take the rest of your cash as a dividend ($4,000 in dividends less the $180 in taxes). That's $3,820 added to your unearned income. You have now brought home $42,167 which leaves you in the 15% tax bracket and you only have to pay $573 more in personal taxes.

Your C-corporation paid $180 in corporate taxes and you paid $573 in personal taxes. This means you actually paid less than 1% in income taxes on the extra $100,000 of income you had beneficial use of. You have $9,000 in a pension plan you can soon borrow against tax-free, paid medical (if you need it), a brand-new car, the best computer system money can buy, trips galore, an assistant at your beck and call, and the $753 in taxes you paid on all of this is more than covered by the $3,820 you received as a dividend.

The important thing to remember is that by using two corporations you paid $8,192 less in taxes earning $175,000 than you paid when making $75,000 as a sole proprietor. Now that is food for thought!

2

DUAL CORPORATION STRATEGY CHART (LESS TAXES)

	Sole Prop. vs.	You + S-Corp. and	C-Corp.
Gross Income	$75,000	$ 65,000	$110,000
Salary	$75,000	$ 8,000	$10,000
Dividend Received		$ 3,820	$ 4,000
Expenses	$10,000	$ 10,000	$100,000
Total Tax	$18,699		$10,507
After-Tax Income	$46,301		$68,493

You may not spend the money the same way as we did in this example, but after reviewing the rest of this book, you should be able to find expenditures you would have chosen to make instead.

The idea is that a sole proprietor has to pay many expenses with after-tax dollars. By using the regular C-corporation, many of these expenses can be paid for with pre-tax dollars. However you pay for them, these expenses are necessary to run your business. The question is, which way would you like to pay for them? Could you afford them at all if you had to pay much more in taxes as a sole proprietor?

You also could choose to pay the marketing corporation up to $30,000 less for its services out of your S-corporation. You could bring that amount home as unearned income and you would still pay less taxes on $175,000 than you would have paid as a sole proprietor on $75,000.

2

DUAL CORPORATION CHART
(MORE INCOME)

	Sole Prop. vs.	You + S-Corp. and	C-Corp.
Gross Income	$75,000	$95,000	$80,000
Salary	$75,000	$ 8,000	$10,000
Dividend Received		$ 3,820	$ 4,000
Expenses	$10,000	$10,000	$70,000
Total Tax	$18,699	$18,334	
After-Tax Income	$46,301	$90,486	

The advantages of incorporating under today's tax laws are clear. Incorporating gives you flexibility. It allows you to structure income in such a way that it is taxed to the least extent the law allows. It allows you to split income, to take advantage of perks and deductions available only to corporations, to plan and save. Today's tax laws don't have to increase your taxes or mean you will pay the same taxes as everyone else. There are legal loopholes, planning tools, and new opportunities in this tax plan.

Take advantage of using corporations to reduce your tax liability. I hope we've given you a clear idea of some of the rules and that you will be able to take advantage of them. When you take advantage of the opportunities available to you, you will not only survive the 21st century, you'll prosper.

2

In the coming pages, we'll discuss some of the unique opportunities available to you for saving tax dollars when you incorporate. We'll discuss some resources available to some corporations that are not available to anyone else. When you are finished reading this, you'll know how to use corporations successfully to put money in your pocket. After all, isn't that what business is all about, making a profit?

Income Splitting			
Taxable Income	No Corporation Married, Filing Jointly* Total Income Tax	One Corporation Married, Filing Jointly* Total Income Tax	Savings
$100,000	$22,124	$15,615	$6,509
$150,000	$37,347	$28,874	$8,473
$200,000	$54,524	$43,346	$11,178
$250,000	$72,524	$59,596	$12,928
$300,000	$90,621	$76,774	$13,847
$350,000	$110,421	$94,774	$15,647
$400,000	$130,221	$112,855	$17,366
$450,000	$150,021	$132,355	$17,666
$500,000	$169,821	$151,855	$17,966

* Assume standard deduction and total of two dependency exemptions.

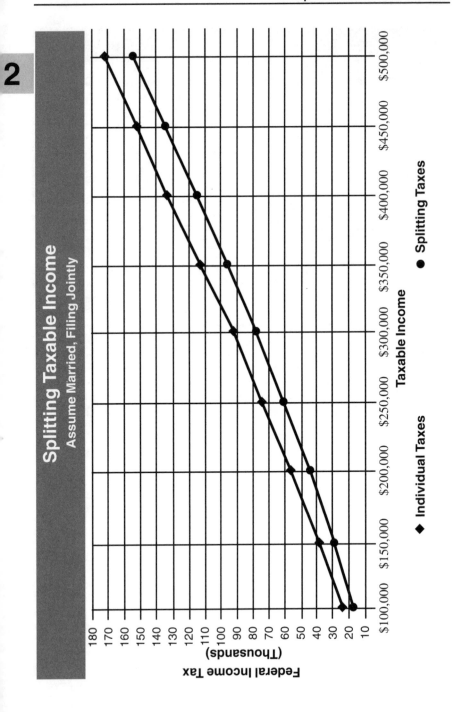

Splitting Taxable Income
Assume Married, Filing Jointly

◆ Individual Taxes   ● Splitting Taxes

Total Taxable Income	Married Filing Jointly* No Corporation Total Income Tax	Married, Filing Jointly with 2 Corporations that are not part of a Controlled Group Total Income Tax	Savings	Savings %
Income Splitting				2
Two Corporations				
$100,000	$22,494	$13,125	$9,369	41.7
$150,000	$37,863	$20,625	$17,238	45.5
$200,000	$55,628	$32,640	$22,988	41.3
$250,000	$73,628	$46,938	$26,690	36.2
$300,000	$92,403	$62,658	$29,745	32.2
$350,000	$111,903	$77,977	$33,926	30.3
$400,000	$131,403	$95,628	$35,775	27.2
$450,000	$151,804	$113,628	$38,176	25.1
$500,000	$171,604	$131,900	$39,704	23.1

*Assume standard deduction and a total of two dependency exemptions.

■ 233 Corporate Tax-Free Deductions

Accounting Fees

Advertising
    Artwork
    Booklets
    Brochures
    Business Cards
    Calendars
    Catalogs
    Design Work
    Fliers
    Graphic Work
    Leaflets
    Matchbooks
    Newspapers
    Radio
    Signs
    Telephone Yellow Pages
    TV
    Typesetting

Air Conditioning

Airplanes
    Leasing
    Maintenance
    Pilot (plus training)
    Purchases

Ammunition
    (corporate security)

Assistants

2

Automobile (leased or owned)
    Accessories
    Anti-Freeze
    Car Washes
    Chains
    Citizen Band Radios
    Depreciation
    Gasoline
    Insurance
    Interest
    License Plates
    Lubrication
    Oil
    Parking
    Registration
    Repairs and Maintenance
    Snow Tires
    Taxes
    Tires
    Tolls

Babysitting (business emergency)

Bad Debts
    (also consider corporation's debt to you)

Baseball Team Equipment
    (business publicity)

Boat(s)

Bonuses

Bookkeeping Expense

Books

2

Bowling Team Sponsorship
(publicity or public relations)

Burglar Alarm Systems

Business Awards and Prizes Given
to Customers

Business Consultants

Business Licenses

Business Seminars

Cables

Calendars

Carbon Paper

Carpentry

Cassettes

Certified Audits

Charitable Contributions
(your church, United Fund, etc.)

Cleaning

Club Memberships

Commission Paid to Salespeople

2

Contract Labor

Contribution to Profit Sharing

Convention Expense

Copyrights

Courses

Decorating

70% Deduction Dividend Income from Stock Owned by Corporation Instead of Individual

Depletion

Depreciation

Directors' Fees

Disability Plans

Discounts to Customers

Drawings

Dues to Professional Organizations

Electrical Bills

Electrical Repairs

Entertainment (80% deductible)
    Ball Games

2

Beverages
Breakfast
Cruises
Hotel Shows
Lunches
Night Club
Theatre

Entertainment at Home to Advance
Corporate Business

Factoring Cost of Receivables

File Cabinets

File Folders

File Hangers

Filing Expense

Financial Consultants

Finder's Fees

Fire Arms (corporate security)

Fire Losses and Flood Losses

Fuel

Gas

General Business Insurance

Gifts as Business Incentives

Gifts to Customers

Health and Accident Insurance

Heat

Helpers

Hurricane Losses

Incorporating Costs

Interest

Internet Service

Invoicing

Jumpsuits

Kitchen Repairs (corporate)

Kitchen Supplies (corporate)

Landscaping

Legal Fees

Life Insurance

Lighting

Limited Partnership Costs

Lobbying Expense

2

Local Transportation

Logo(s)

Losses In Business

Losses on Sale or Exchanges of Capital Assets

Machinery and Equipment

Magazines

Mailgrams

Maintenance

Masonry

Medical Reimbursement Plan
    Acupuncture
    Alcoholism Treatment
    Ambulance
    Anesthetist
    Artificial Limb or Teeth
    Blood Donor

Meetings at Resort or Luxury Hotels

Messenger Service

Miscellaneous Expenses

Moving Expense

Moving Expenses Paid to Employee

2

Chiropodist
Chiropractor
Christian Science Practitioner Fees
Clinic
Contact Lenses and Upkeep
Crutches and Braces
Diathermy
Doctor (all types) and Dental Fees
Eyeglasses
Fees to Doctor
Gynecologist
Hearing Aids and their Upkeep
Heart Surgery
Legal Vasectomy
Midwife
Obstetrician
Oculist
Optometrist
Osteopath
Pediatrician
Podiatrist
Prescribed Birth Control and
    Devices
Sanitarium
Surgeon

Hospital Expenses (not reimbursed)
    Air Conditioning
    Busses or Mileage if You Own a
      Car
    Drugs and Medicine
    Health Clubs
    Lab Fees
    Nursing Services (including board)
    Prescribed Items by Doctors
    Psychiatric Fees

2

Special Equipment
Special Foods
Taxis
Therapy
Transportation for Medical Care
Trips
Vitamins and Minerals
Wheel chairs
X-Rays

Newsletters

Newspapers

Office Construction

Office Expenses

Office Purchases

Office Rental

Pads

Paper

Paper Clips

Part-Time Help

Passport Fees

Patents

Payroll Taxes

2

Pencils

Pens

Pension Plans

Planting

Plumbing

Postage

Printing
    Ads
    Books
    Brochures
    Business Cards
    Stationery

Professional Fees

Public Relations Items
        football teams,
        bands, etc.

Professional Literature

Records

Refuse Collection

Retreats for Corporate Meetings,
Seminars or Bonuses

Roofing

2

Sprinkler System

Staples

Safe Deposit Box Rental

Telegrams

Telephone Calls

Theft Losses

Tips and Gratuities

Tools

Trademarks

Training Programs and Compensation
(which can be for your children
 and other family members if employed)

Travel (anywhere on business)

Trucks

Uniform Cost and Cleaning (Uniforms can
mean many variations of clothing not normally thought of as a uniform as long as it is
specifically required dress by the employer
and cannot be worn for everyday use.)

University (If required to maintain or improve required skills or if required by corporation.)

Victory Celebrations for Achieving Corporate Goals and Objectives

Wages and Consulting Fees (This can include members of your family.)

Water

Wires

Worker's Compensation Insurance

Worthless Securities

2

2 Lawsuit-proof Your Business While You Reduce State Income Taxes

Corporations are very valuable and flexible tools, yet we have only scratched the surface so far. What if you could limit your liability from lawsuits by judgment-proofing your assets and significantly reduce or even eliminate state income taxes?

The strategy discussed below takes advantage of two powerful features of corporations:

1. Corporations are considered independent legal entities, separate from their owners.

2. Corporations can be based in any state regardless of where their owners live.

By taking advantage of these two features, it is possible to make yourself lawsuit-proof and/or legally eliminate state income taxes.

The best liability insurance anybody could have is to be completely poverty stricken and destitute. We also know that if you never make a profit in your home state, then you will owe no income tax to

2

your home state— if your state defines taxable income as net earnings and profit. (The exception is an income tax based on gross income.) The principles behind this strategy are two companies doing business together.

Here are the steps you need to take.

1. Incorporate the home state business you currently derive income from. For purposes of this example, we are going to call your home state corporation "Red, Inc." That's because your home state operation will have a lot of red ink. It will

> *"The best liability insurance anyone could have is to be completely poverty stricken and destitute."*

try to make a profit, but when it ends up with red ink (losing money), there will be no state income taxes to pay. Consider making it an S-corporation and elect a tax year ending December 31.

2. Set up another corporation in a state that has no state income tax, such as Nevada. For purposes of this example, we will call this corporation "Warbucks, Inc." Elect a fiscal year ending June 30 for it.

2

3. Operating in your home state, Red, Inc. decides it would be a fine idea to buy some products and/or services from Warbucks, Inc. Remember, Red, Inc. and Warbucks, Inc. are separate corporations and therefore separate persons (a corporation is "an artifical person created by law"). Therefore, if Red, Inc. writes a check to Warbucks, Inc., money is spent by Red, Inc. (your home- state-based person) and money is received by Warbucks, Inc. (your tax-free-state- based person). There is an expense in your home state to Red, Inc. and there is income to Warbucks, Inc. If Red, Inc. spends all its profits, it makes no money for your home state to tax—plus you have an excellent lawsuit-proofing tool which we'll explain later.

Just what products and services can Warbucks, Inc. sell to Red, Inc. from the tax-free state and still not be liable for state taxes in your home state? What we suggest as the most solid and workable option is that Warbucks, Inc. simply loan money to Red, Inc., which would simply be buying the use of money from Warbucks, Inc. When you borrow money, you generally pay interest. Red, Inc. is no exception. You put money into Warbucks, Inc., which uses the money that has been invested in it to make money. It does this by loaning money to Red, Inc. (and preferably others as well).

The condition of the loan to Red, Inc. is that the money owed is due and payable whenever Warbucks, Inc. asks for it ("calls the note"). This kind of note is called a "demand promissory note."

2

Also, as any good business does, Warbucks, Inc. charges Red, Inc. (your home state operation) interest on the money it has loaned. Be sure to check the usury laws for the state Warbucks, Inc. is located in. For this example, we'll say the rate is 18%. The interest may be due monthly or annually and it may even be compounded monthly. This will get Red, Inc. even further in debt to Warbucks, Inc., which can be very beneficial as you'll see later.

To summarize so far, Red, Inc. borrows money from Warbucks, Inc. with the principal balance due upon demand (when Warbucks, Inc. calls the note). The money owed to Warbucks, Inc. is evidenced by a promissory note written by Red, Inc. (the debtor) at the offices of Warbucks, Inc. This note shows that the money is borrowed in Warbuck's home state and, if worded correctly, that it is governed by the laws of that state. How much does Red, Inc. borrow from Warbucks, Inc.? Well, at 18% simple interest (used only by way of example), if Red, Inc. borrowed $100,000, this would mean a business interest expense to Red, Inc. in your home state of $18,000 in one year. It could be more if the interest compounded monthly.

2

Depending upon the amount of money borrowed and the interest rate the two companies (which you own) agree upon, the interest expense to Red, Inc. in your home state could be higher or lower.

Note: This strategy works just as well if you sell products and/or services to Red, Inc. instead of lending it money. Warbucks, Inc. sells the products and services to Red, Inc. and takes back a promissory note. Interest on the note is due monthly or yearly. The interest is still an expense to Red, Inc. and the result is the same; no profit for Red, Inc. in your home state. The principal amount of the note may also be deductible to Red, Inc.

■ Lawsuit-Proof

The stage is now set. All that remains are a few simple steps to make your business operation lawsuit-proof.

Warbucks, Inc. is based outside of your home state and it maintains a low profile. Its main client is Red, Inc. which you own. The chances of Warbucks, Inc. getting sued are slim to none.

The idea is to make Red, Inc. lawsuit-proof by turning it into a turnip that no one can bleed for money. At the same time, you need to make sure it has the money, equipment, fixtures, land, buildings, etc. to conduct your business. Here are the steps.

First, create a large debt. Red, Inc. borrows money from Warbucks, Inc. every time it gets a chance. It probably even finances part of its interest payments to Warbucks, Inc. because it can't make them all in cash. Therefore, each month the debt keeps increasing. It would not be hard to establish a debt so large to Warbucks, Inc. that it exceeds the value of all the assets of Red, Inc.

2

Let's say Red, Inc. has assets totaling $250,000 that you want to protect. Red, Inc. borrows and borrows from Warbucks, Inc. getting deeper and deeper in debt. The debt figure is limited only by the principal amount Warbucks, Inc. and Red, Inc. agree upon and the corresponding interest rate.

"If Red, Inc. spends all of its profits, it makes no money for your home state to tax..."

"Warbucks, Inc. is in first position on all of the assets that Red, Inc. owns and those assets can't be touched until Warbucks, Inc. is paid."

2

Next, draw up a "security agreement." Warbucks, Inc. is going to make sure it gets paid. It will want some collateral on the loan to Red, Inc. A security agreement is a common, powerful tool that is used to secure certain assets as collateral on a loan. By this agreement, Warbucks, Inc. and Red, Inc. agree that the assets, receivables, inventory and everything belonging to Red, Inc. are collateral for the loan. On any equity in real property, Red, Inc. would issue a deed of trust (mortgage) to Warbucks, Inc.

Then file a "UCC-1." As notice to the world that these assets are collateral for a debt owed to Warbucks, Inc., Warbucks, Inc. will record what is called a "UCC-1" financing statement with the Secretary of State's office and/or appropriate County Recorders Office in your home state. The UCC-1 form states that these assets are collateral for a note that is owed. It gives notice to the world that these assets are encumbered and no one can touch these assets until the debt owed to Warbucks, Inc. is paid.

Warbucks, Inc. is in first position on all of the assets that Red, Inc. owns and those assets can't be touched until Warbucks, Inc. is paid. UCC-1 filings and the security agreement, which perfects a security interest in the assets of Red, Inc., come before everything else (except some tax claims). In other words, this is correct unless other creditors have filed liens or perfected their security interests prior to your filing the UCC-1.

2

What happens if Red, Inc. gets sued? When the lawyer and the person suing Red, Inc. check on the assets owned by Red, Inc., they get a very rude awakening. They search to see what Red, Inc. is worth, which includes looking for any real property it owns along with any debt against it, and any UCC-1 filings encumbering the assets Red, Inc. may own. They find a big debt. They find that all of the assets of Red, Inc. are encumbered and that Red, Inc. is worthless. That's probably the end of the lawsuit against Red, Inc.

However, let's say that person decides to sue and files the lawsuit. He even gets a judgment against Red, Inc.

Remember, Warbucks, Inc. is owed money by Red, Inc., as evidenced by a promissory note due on demand. Warbucks, Inc. decides it is time to get paid and calls the note. Red, Inc. can't pay such a large debt. Warbucks, Inc. has no recourse except to execute its security interest and/or deed of trust on the assets of Red, Inc. by taking the assets of Red, Inc. to satisfy the debt.

What happened? That's the same question the attorney who sued you is asking. He's got a judgment against Red, Inc. but Red, Inc. has nothing to execute that judgment on. In fact, you could even call the attorney and tell him, "I'll give you the whole corporation. Come on down and pick up the keys." Even though Warbucks, Inc. has taken the assets of Red, Inc., the debt owed to Warbucks, Inc. may be so large that Red, Inc. still owes money to Warbucks, Inc.

2

In that case, the only thing your opponent would gain is a large debt owed to Warbucks, Inc.— which you own.

To reiterate what we've just discussed, here's a summary of the steps to lawsuit-proof Red, Inc.

1. Warbucks, Inc. loans money to Red, Inc.

2. The money Red, Inc. owes Warbucks, Inc. is evidenced by a promissory note due when Warbucks, Inc. says it's due.

3. As security or collateral, Warbucks, Inc. and Red, Inc. agree that the assets of Red, Inc. will be collateral and security for the note.

4. As notice to the world and evidence that these assets are collateral on the loan, a UCC-1 filing is done in Warbuck's home state and in your home state. A trust deed is executed on any real property and filed in the county in which said property is located.

5. Warbucks, Inc. is in first position on the assets of Red, Inc. and no one who may sue Red, Inc. can touch those assets until the debt to Warbucks, Inc. is paid.

6. You are doing business "lawsuit-proof" because even if there is a judgment against Red, Inc., there is nothing to take.

Review the diagram on the following page. If you have any questions or if you need assistance setting up your Warbucks/Red, Inc. strategy, call us at 1-800-648-0966 for a free consultation.

How to Eliminate your State Income Tax and be Lawsuit-Proof

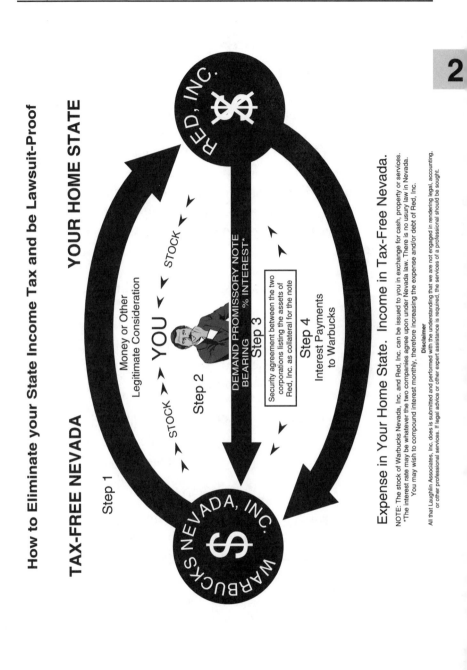

TAX-FREE NEVADA

YOUR HOME STATE

RED, INC.

WARBUCKS NEVADA, INC.

Step 1

Money or Other
Legitimate Consideration

STOCK >> **YOU** << STOCK

STOCK

Step 2

DEMAND PROMISSORY NOTE
BEARING ___ % INTEREST*

Step 3

Security agreement between the two
corporations listing the assets of
Red, Inc. as collateral for the note

Step 4

Interest Payments
to Warbucks

Expense in Your Home State. Income in Tax-Free Nevada.

NOTE: The stock of Warbucks Nevada, Inc. and Red, Inc. can be issued to you in exchange for cash, property or services. *The interest rate may be whatever the two companies agree upon under Nevada law. There is no usury law in Nevada. You may wish to compound interest monthly, therefore increasing the expense and/or debt of Red, Inc.

Disclaimer
All that Laughlin Associates, Inc. does is submitted and performed with the understanding that we are not engaged in rendering legal, accounting, or other professional services. If legal advice or other expert assistance is required, the services of a professional should be sought.

Which State Is Right For You?

One of the first choices you have to make upon deciding to incorporate involves selecting the proper state of incorporation. Since you are not required to incorporate in the state where your business will primarily operate, you can choose from any one of the 50 states. A number of important factors must be weighed to make the proper choice.

1. The location of your physical facilities.

2. A cost analysis comparing incorporating in the state of operation versus qualifying to do business as a foreign corporation (out-of-state corporation).

3. Determining the advantages and disadvantages of each state's corporate laws, tax structure and privacy orientation.

4. Your personal financial goals. What benefits are you seeking? Are you primarily concerned with liability protecttion, tax savings, privacy, or a combination of all three?

Let's make it simple. If your intention is to conduct business in a specific state—usually the one where you live or where your operating facilities are located—that usually is the best state in which to incorporate. You'll enjoy limited liability protection, receive benefits not available to sole proprietors or partnerships, and profit from a choice of tax situations.

2

If, on the other hand, you are already incorporated in your home state or wish to create a second entity for purposes of income splitting, protecting assets, building a firewall of financial privacy and want to significantly reduce or completely eliminate your state income taxes, you might consider incorporating in a "preferred state" such as Nevada or Wyoming.

■ When And Why To Incorporate In Your Home State: Pros And Cons

When and under what circumstances do you want to incorporate in your home state? Why would you want to incorporate in a state that you don't live in or do business in? Those questions can seem complex. Like most complex questions, the answers or solutions are simple when the subject is understood and the facts assembled.

Keep in mind that our purpose is to take the mystery out of corporations and their use, to strip them of unnecessary complexities, to make them simple so all can benefit. So, where should you incorporate?

2

Although there are many cases when you are better off to incorporate in your home state, there are also many times when you should incorporate outside. You should know the pros and cons of each alternative.

A corporation is a citizen of the state where it was created. A corporation does not cease to be a citizen of the state in which it is incorporated by engaging in business or acquiring property in another state.

For example, you are a citizen of the United States. When you go into Mexico or Canada, you do not lose your citizenship but you do become subject to the laws and taxes in Mexico or Canada. However, since you are a United States citizen, you have certain rights as a result of that citizenship and you also have the right to return to the United States.

That is one valid, valuable reason why it is often wise to incorporate in the state with the best corporation and tax laws regardless of where you are going to do business. If for any reason you ever need to, you do have a safe haven to which you can return, retreat or withdraw.

As a side note, one of the benefits to incorporating in a preferred state is that, regardless of where the corporation does business, its inner workings are governed by the state of incorporation.

■ When To Incorporate In Your Home State

2

If, for example, you are starting a small retail business in your home state and you never intend the business to become involved in interstate operations or sales, then you are probably well-advised to incorporate in your home state.

Many people mistakenly believe that they can form a corporation elsewhere and simply proceed to do business wherever they are. That is usually not true because each state has exceptions to its legal definition of "doing business within that state." You should find out what the legal definition and exceptions are in your state.

If the law in your home state legally defines your activities as doing business within that state, then you must either incorporate in your home state or qualify your out-of-state corporation to do business in your home state. Simply having formed a corporation somewhere else does not necessarily permit you to do business everywhere without either qualifying to do business in each additional state or being legally exempt from qualifying or registering.

You should ask your attorney or possibly your Secretary of State's office what constitutes doing business in your state. You must determine what the exemptions are in your own state in order to know whether your activities constitute transacting business within your state.

2

For example, in most states, a corporation can own property in any other state without having to qualify there. Therefore, in owning or buying real property, you are exempt from incorporating or qualifying to do business in your home state. When that circumstance exists, you may instead want to incorporate in a preferred state and let that corporation own the property.

If activities of your business require you to qualify in your home state, then you must make the decision whether it is best to incorporate in your home state or to incorporate in a more business friendly state and qualify to do business in your state. It is an important decision and you should consider it carefully.

Stock Dividends!
Save! Save! Save!

■ What Is The Best Way?

By having your corporation own stock and receive
the dividends, you save money while maintaining
total control.

■ How Does This Work?

A corporation is entitled to a deduction from its gross
income for the dividends it receives from domestic
corporations it owns an interest in. If your corporation owns less than 20% of the stock of the corporation paying the dividends, the exclusion is 70% of
the dividends that are received. Only 30% of what
is actually received is taxable. If your corporation
owns at least 20% but less than 80% of the stock of
the corporation paying the dividends, the exclusion
increases to 80% of the dividends received. You
pay tax on only 20%. Finally, if your corporation
owns 80% or more of the shares of the paying corporation, the deduction is 100%. No tax. As you
can see, this is a huge benefit for anyone who owns
dividend-producing stock. This little-known wealth
shelter can increase your yield substantially.

How To Win A Losing Proposition

2

There is a man who races go-carts. Each year, he would spend money and not get a dime's worth of tax benefit out of it. Nowadays, he sells advertising on his go-carts to businesses that pay him to race his go-carts. Unfortunately, or as it turns out, fortunately, he hasn't made a profit yet. There is no law against being stupid. He tries hard, because in order to be a business you have to try to make a profit, but he just can't seem to do it. He's made business expenses out of what would otherwise be personal expenses. Now he gets a tax refund check at the end of each year.

An S-corporation can work well for people like this. The reason is that an S-corporation really pays no taxes. It passes through its losses to you, its shareholder. If an S-corporation has net income, it also passes through to its individual shareholder as well. So if you incorporate a hobby and make it a for-profit business and that S-corporation business loses money, you get the benefit of a tax deduction that could result in a refund check. Take a look at which of your personal expenses could be turned into business expenses and you might save a bundle.

■ How to Make an S-Corporation Work for You

2

Everybody hears a lot about S-corporations being the tax haven of today. While no business exists solely for the purpose of being a tax deduction, any business trying to make a profit can lose money instead. Here's how it works.

1. First, you incorporate.

2. Then the corporation acquires for business purposes, of course, various and sundry assets such as a company car, yacht, and airplane. There is nothing new about any of this.

3. These assets cost a lot of money and they cost a lot to license, insure, operate, maintain, garage, dock, and hangar. This expense is all necessary to the conduct and pursuit of the corporation's business, in the judgment of the corporation, and it is reflected in the corporate record book in the form of resolutions or minutes. That judgment may be good or bad, successful or unsuccessful, profitable or unprofitable, and it may go on for up to five years.

   The corporation continues trying to make a profit.

2

If it is unprofitable and the corporation loses money, the corporation obviously has a loss. That loss, under S-corporation status, is a direct deduction from your personal 1040 federal income tax return, up to whatever amount you have invested in the corporation! You have just made or saved money!

That's why the law is there. Congress created subchapter S to eliminate certain unfairness they saw to small business people under the old rules. Don't fail to take advantage of the opportunity the government has created for you.

4. There are many other expenses the corporation may have which can also result in more losses to the corporation and more personal tax deductions for you. Some examples are office rent, telephone bills, and travel expenses.

5. By now you are probably thinking, "Very good, that's all great but where does this newly-formed corporation get the money it needs to spend on these expenses?

You use the money you otherwise would have spent for those items to purchase stock in the corporation. That money is not taxable to the corporation and it is money you have invested in the corporation.

2

The corporation can then use the money to purchase the assets we talked about in Step 2. If the corporation loses money, then that loss is a deduction for you instead of just money out the window.

6. Under tax regulations, the loss deduction you take from the S-corporation cannot exceed the investment (basis) you have in the ownership (stock) of the S-corporation. So, we suggest you stick to investing money in the corporation's stock through equity investment instead of loaning money to the corporation. By the same plan, lawyer and legal expenses can often be handled through the corporation as corporate expenses instead of personal expenses and thereby become further tax deductions for you.

These are just a few ideas and examples hopefully to stimulate your thinking and show you how to operate an S-corporation. Keep in mind that under S-corporation status, the corporation itself is not taxed. In the event the corporation has a profit, that profit is passed through to your 1040 personal tax return just like the loss we discussed above. This eliminates double taxation, otherwise the profit would be taxed first on the corporate level and again on the individual level when it is received from the corporation.

"If the corporation loses money, then that loss is a deduction for you instead of just money out the window."

2   Write Off Anything The Doctor Orders

■ Tax Savings For The Individual And The Corporation

One of the big advantages of incorporation is the number of benefits that can be paid for with pre-tax dollars. For an individual, these items would normally come out of after-tax income. One of the best is a Medical Reimbursement Plan (MRP) which pays all of an employee's medical expenses. The expenses for the MRP are tax deductible by the corporation and are not considered to be income for the employee.

For example, an individual's medical expenses are only deductible to the extent that the total exceeds 7.5% of his adjusted gross income. If the individual earns $40,000, for example, then the first $3,000 of medical expenses are not deductible. If that individual worked for a corporation with an MRP, then that same $3,000 would be paid tax-free to the corporation and receive a 100% tax write-off of this amount.

In order to qualify, an MRP must be formally established by the corporation's Board of Directors. It must primarily be for the benefit of the employees. Certainly, you can be an employee of your own corporation. The MRP can be very flexible since there is no requirement for minimum or maximum amounts to be allocated to the plan during any given period and there are no regular premiums to be paid since it is not insurance.

A corporation can design its own MRP by using ready-made forms or with the aid of lawyers and benefits consultants. The MRP allows the corporation to pay the medical expenses of its employees and their dependents and to deduct those payments from its taxable income. In turn, the employee's do not include those payments in their taxable income. An MRP is usually designed to apply only to current employees and it can be terminated upon written notice to those employees who are covered.

■ Creative Applications

Any medical service, product or appliance which is used "to improve the employee's health" is a candidate for payment under an MRP. Any procedure, medication or appliance recommended by a doctor or health specialist can be covered. This allows for a great deal of flexibility and creativity.

2

Some examples of tax deductions which have been allowed under MRPs include:

Clarinet Lessons. An employee received non-taxed funds from the MRP account for the cost of a clarinet and lessons that were recommended by an orthodontist to correct a child's bite (Revenue Ruling 62-210).

New Siding. The cost of replacing moldy shingles was paid from the MRP account to an employee whose wife was susceptible to nasal infections. Her doctor advised the replacement of the shingles which permitted dust and mold irritants to enter the house (Revenue Ruling 8112089).

Paint Removal. A child developed lead poisoning after licking lead-based paint on the exterior of his parent's house. The cost of removing the paint and its replacement with non-lead house paint was ruled to be a valid reimbursement from the MRP (Revenue Ruling 79-66).

Elevator. An employee's wife was involved in an accident that left her paralyzed and in a wheelchair. An elevator was installed in the house to provide access to the upstairs bedrooms. The total cost was paid out of the MRP.

Hair Transplant. The secretary of a corporation had treatment for cancer which left her balding. The MRP paid for wigs and hair transplants to restore hair loss due to the medical treatments.

■ Broader Coverage

An MRP can provide broader medical coverage than standard major medical insurance plans without the hassles of allowable versus non-allowable expenditures that most insurance plans perpetrate upon employees. At the same time, they provide a place to keep earned, undistributed income for the corporation.

2

■ MRPs Must Not Discriminate

Medical Reimbursement Plans, because they are a form of a self-insured health plan, must be non-discriminatory. This means that they must not discriminate in favor of "highly compensated employees" who are defined as employees who:

1. Are among the five highest paid officers of the company,
2. Or more than 10% of the shares of the company;
3. Or among the highest-paid 25% of all employees other than officers.

In addition, the MRP must benefit:

1. Seventy percent or more of all employees,
2. Eighty percent or more of all employees who are eligible to participate.

Employees who need not be considered when making the above calculations include:

1. Employees with less than three years of service,

2

2. Employees who are under 25 years of age,
3. Employees with part-time or seasonable jobs,
4. Employees who are non-resident aliens,
5. Employees who are union members.

■ The Como Strategy

Ray Como, an entrepreneur and corporate strategist, has suggested an ingenious way to take advantage of MRPs to cut a corporation's normal health insurance costs by up to 80%. The idea is startling in its simplicity. Rather than take health coverage with the normal small deductible (usually $100 or $250), the corporation takes the maximum deductible—usually around $2,500. This cuts the cost per employee from around $300 down to around $50 per month. The corporation then allocates enough funds to an MRP to cover its $2,500 per person deductible exposure.

The beauty of this strategy is that:

1. The funds paid under the MRP are fully deductible by the corporation,

2. Unlike insurance premiums, the funds in the MRP are only paid out on an as-needed basis and accumulate interest for the corporation until they are required.

The corporation can take two approaches to funding the MRP. It can fund the entire $2,500 for each employee (with full knowledge that only a small percentage of that amount is likely to be required) and the remaining funds become, in effect, tax-deferred income to the corporation. Or, it can calculate the amount of funding likely to be required to meet each employee's requirements and supply this minimum funding. Either way, the corporation's medical plan expenses are likely to be considerably reduced and its cash flow dramatically enhanced by this creative approach to benefit funding.

2

2

Double Taxation—What It Is and How To Avoid It

Many will say, "Sure, corporations pay less tax up to $110,656 in net taxable income but the income that corporations do receive is double-taxed, so this benefit is really no benefit at all." Well, that is true if you do everything wrong. If you form a corporation, earn income, take advantage of only a handful of deductions available to it, take advantage of fringe benefits, and declare all income that the corporation receives as a dividend to the shareholders, then this statement has a lot of merit.

Instead, look at what happens when you do a few things right.

First, people who say the income a corporation receives is double-taxed assume that the shareholders are going to take the income out in the form of dividends. You see, a corporation pays taxes separately from its shareholders, assuming it's not an S-corporation—which generally doesn't pay taxes (its shareholders do, so there is no double tax problem in an S-corporation). When a regular corporation earns money, it pays taxes on its net income. When a regular corporation pays a dividend to its shareholders, it cannot deduct that dividend. However, when a shareholder receives a dividend, he must pay tax on it.

That means that the same income was taxed once at the corporate level and again at the individual level. This costs a lot of money and is done only as a last resort for taking money out of a corporation.

2

There's no law that says a corporation must distribute its profits to its shareholders in the form of dividends. Many people seem to think there is. A corporation does not have to declare a dividend. It can simply retain the earnings in the corporation. That way the money is only taxed once. Furthermore, since a corporation pays less tax on its income up to $110,656 net, the income is not only taxed just once but the corporation also pays less tax as an individual would have. You save money.

Not only that but the corporation has many more deductions available to it than does an individual. So, a corporation can earn much more than an individual and still pay less tax.

Maybe you've heard your accountant say that there is a limitation on how much money a corporation can retain without declaring a dividend. Well, it depends. The corporation can retain up to $250,000 without ever having to declare a dividend. Many people will tell you that when retained income reaches $250,000 it must declare a dividend. That is not true. The corporation can retain far in excess of $250,000 provided it is retaining that income for growth and has a corporate resolution to that effect. Most businesses want to grow, don't they?

2

Many people operate under the assumption that they have to take money out of their corporation. This just isn't true. When you have a corporation, you have a corporate checkbook. It is just as easy to write a check on the corporation as it is to write one out of your personal checkbook. Most things that a person wants to write a check for can easily be justified as business expenses. The corporation can buy a car, pay medical expenses, provide for an individual's retirement, buy real estate, or even buy an airplane. Let the corporation do it. Why take the money out?

Well, you say, you want to spend some money on wine and song and then spend the rest foolishly. Okay, while some of the wine and song can probably be written off as corporate entertainment expense, much of it probably can't. So, how do you take money out of your closely-held corporation without using a dividend?

One way is the corporation could loan you the money or you may have loaned the corporation some money when you first started out and the corporation is paying you interest payments. In the case of the corporation loaning you money, there is no tax. Of course, you would have to pay the corporation interest on any money you borrow and the corporation would have to claim that as taxable income but the tax effects are minimal. With the lower corporate tax rates and higher corporate deductions, you would still have quite a tax benefit.

2

If you loaned money to the corporation when you started out and the corporation is paying you interest, yes, that interest is income to you and is taxable. But that interest is deductible to the corporation, so you're only taxed once on that money. You've eliminated double taxation. Further, corporate money paid to you as a payment on the principal amount you loaned it is not income to you at all.

Also, the corporation is probably going to pay you a salary of some sort. That salary is an expense to the corporation and income to you. It is not double taxed, except to the extent that the corporation and you must contribute 7.65% each in Social Security taxes. However, the corporation's contribution is a deductible payroll tax expense on the corporation's books, and again, the tax benefits that the corporation provides more than make up for the Social Security tax.

So there you have it. First, there's no law that says the corporation has to declare a dividend to begin with. Second, you probably don't need to take that much money out of the corporation. Third, if you do need to take money out of your corporation, there are much better ways than dividends. As you can see, double taxation is really an overblown problem. In fact, in most closely-held corporations, it is no problem at all.

How To Take Money Out Of A Closely-Held Company

2

Many businessmen today face a common dilemma: How to safely take money out of their closely-held companies for their own support while keeping the business financially healthy. There are many ways to do this because tax laws let you spread income among family members in lower tax brackets. You can legally avoid high bracket taxes.

Often the easiest and quickest way for a successful business person to save tax dollars is to incorporate. How can incorporating help save tax dollars? Some examples follow.

1. Corporate tax rates are lower than corresponding individual rates up to about $173,000 in taxable income. Therefore, you can save on taxes by directing as much of your income as possible into your corporation.

2. A salary for services is the most obvious way to get money from your corporation. The payment to you by the corporation is deductible to the corporation. Be careful, though, that you don't take too much out as salary. If your salary is questioned by the IRS and found to be too much for the tasks you perform in relation to the overall income of the corporation, deductibility of your salary will be denied. You will still get the same amount of income, but

2

the corporation will not be able to deduct the payments. It will be considered
a dividend payment and will be taxed to
the corporation nevermind that you will
be taxed on it personally as well. One
way to get around the unreasonableness
issue is to have a smaller salary and provide for bonuses, both short and long-
term, based on company profitability.
Your employment contract with the corporation (you do have one, don't you?)
should set out the terms of your employment, benefits, vacation, salary, bonuses,
etc., particularly if you are a shareholder.

3. Current fringe benefits are tax-free to the
corporation's employees, and they are deductible expenses for the corporation.
Health, disability, and life insurance, tuition
help for students, special executive training,
and travel to conventions are only a few
fringes with helpful tax benefits for both the
corporation and its employees. Instead of
getting a paycheck and buying such services
with after-tax dollars, you're getting your services paid with before-tax dollars. The payments are tax deductible by the corporation
and are not included in your income. Also
included here are company automobiles, airplanes, condominiums, and so on.

4. Utilize deferred fringe benefits. The corporation gets a deduction for its contribution to pension and profit-sharing plans,
while you get the funds in a tax-free trust

2

for your retirement. Corporations have access to other types of non-qualified employee benefit plans with far fewer restrictions than traditional IRAs or Keogh plans.

5. Shareholders may arrange for interest-bearing loans from the corporation. To make this work offer proof that the loan was not a gift by arranging for periodic repayment of the interest.

6. Leasing, not purchasing, may save you tax dollars. A family partnership may purchase property and lease it to the corporation at a fair price. The corporation deducts the rent it pays to the partnership as a business expense. The makeup of the partnership is also important. Taxpayers in higher brackets should be involved if the partnership can show a loss. Taxpayers in lower brackets who can absorb a gain should be involved if the partnership is making solid income.

7. A corporation with high past earnings, a promising future, and no plan to invest its earnings may choose to file an S-corporation election. This passes any gain or loss directly through to individual taxpayers and avoids the double taxation otherwise encountered by a corporation and its shareholders.

8. Another concept is to have your spouse and children on the payroll. Their pay must

be reasonable for the work performed, but this can be easily accomplished. Often even young children can do office cleaning and janitorial duties, run errands, and answer telephones. Almost certainly their tax rates are going to be less than yours, and you won't have to give them an allowance.

2

Your Retirement And Social Security Benefits

Almost everybody has to pay into Social Security; but we all know as time goes on, that the benefits received from Social Security will continue to dwindle and we must look to other means to maximize our retirement. Social Security regulations are changing. As more people are trying to take advantage of early retirement, the regulations become stricter; but as people continue to work past the age of 65, the regulations allow for full benefits even if you continue to receive other sources of income.

If you take early retirement (before 65), you are only eligible to receive $10,080 a year. If you exceed $10,080 through supplemental income, you will be penalized $1 in benefits for every $2 you earn. In the year you turn full retirement age, $1 in benefits will be deducted for every $3 you earn above $17,000. Starting with the month you reach full retirement age, benefits will be allotted with NO LIMIT on your earnings. These new rules apply for the entire year of 2000, beginning in January.

2

There is a way to take advantage of early retirement and still receive your maximum Social Security benefits. The amount of Social Security benefits an individual can receive without being penalized for additional income is based on reportable income. Reportable income includes commissions, wages, fees, vacation pay, severance pay, and tips. These must be reported annually to the Social Security Administration on HEW Form 777.

There is income you can receive that is not reportable to the Social Security Administration including pensions, veterans benefits, royalties, rental income from real estate, gifts, inheritance, capital gains, annuity income, interest on savings and investment income in the form of dividends. You will still have to pay tax on these unreportable incomes but they do not reduce your monthly Social Security benefits, regardless of how much you make.

CHAPTER 3
SUMMARY

3

Definitions

■ Basic Corporate Definitions

3

Alter ego doctrine—This principle allows the courts to refuse a corporation's right to shield it's owners from the liabilities associated with the corporation. It stipulates that a corporation formed merely for personal advancement not sound and legitimate business purposes—cannot be considered a corporation.

Annual meeting of directors—This is a yearly meeting of the directors of a corporation to show ongoing management of the corporation. These meetings are mandatory and help to prove the corporation is currently viable.

Annual meeting of stockholders—This is a yearly meeting of the stockholders of a corporation to show ongoing management of the corporation. These meetings are mandatory and further help to prove the corporation's viability.

Articles of incorporation—These Articles represent the contracts that hold the corporation together and set the guidelines for the business purpose and how the corporation will be structured.

The above definitions are not intended to be complete legal definitions. If a full definition is desired, please contact us and we will refer you to a qualified source.

Assessable Stock — This is a type of stock that a corporation may issue. A holder of this type of stock is liable for the debts of the corporation up to an amount equal to his percentage of ownership in the corporation.

3

Assets — The assets of a business are property, real or personal, tangible or intangible, that have value.

Audit — An audit is any procedure that scrutinizes and analyzes any part of a process. It is usually associated with the IRS reviewing your records to insure their viability and correctness.

Authorized Stock — Authorized Stock is the maximum amount of stock that the home state will allow you to issue.

Back Dating versus Reconstructing Resolutions — Backdating any document is illegal, as it tries to convey that a document was processed earlier than it actually was. Reconstructing resolutions is a way to document decisions made in the past that a corporation failed to document at that time.

Bearer Shares — Stock of a corporation that is owned by the holder of those shares. These are hard to track and make it hard to call meetings or take a vote in a corporation.

The above definitions are not intended to be complete legal definitions. If a full definition is desired, please contact us and we will refer you to a qualified source.

3

Bylaws — The bylaws of a corporation set the rules by which the corporation is to be run.

Calendar Year — When a corporation sets its fiscal year end date as December 31, it is using the calendar year as its fiscal year.

Capitalization — This term describes the money and assets placed in a corporation to get it started. A corporation will need enough capitalization at all times to insure its future success. Even if a corporation is in debt, if it has the ability to earn, it is not considered undercapitalized.

Consent to Action — This is the formal process by which the stockholders of a corporation set goals and provide direction for the corporation.

Consideration — The object of value given by either party in any agreement.

Controlled Group — A controlled group of corporations is considered a single entity by tax assessors and therefore files a consolidated tax return. S-Corporations are not subject to being considered part of a controlled group.

Corporate Charter — The document provided by the state government that recognizes the existence and start date of a corporation.

Corporate Seal — A seal used by a corporation to show its approval of documents. Although many

The above definitions are not intended to be complete legal definitions. If a full definition is desired, please contact us and we will refer you to a qualified source.

states don't require its use, some do. Use it regardless of your own state's requirements to save you time working in a state that requires its use for its domestic corporations.

3

Corporation — An entity brought into existence through the recognition by the state. It has certain rights, privileges and responsibilities normally associated with individuals. It can live forever, yet it remains a veritable slave to its owners, who share in its profits but are shielded from its losses.

It is a way to structure your business that affords you less personal liability and more tax breaks, by its very design lending itself to strategies that can make you judgement-proof, assure your financial privacy, and you save a small fortune on taxes.

Deed of Trust — A document that evidences a lien on real property, not unlike a mortgage.

Director — An individual selected to sit on a board that transforms the goals of the stockholders into action plans.

Director Committee — A group of Directors and/ or non-directors that focusses on and finds solutions for problems selected by the Board of Directors.

Dividend — A method to disburse profits from a business. These payments are not classified as payments for services and are not subject to payroll taxes. They are considered unearned income.

The above definitions are not intended to be complete legal definitions. If a full definition is desired, please contact us and we will refer you to a qualified source.

3

Doing Business — A set of criteria, which varies from state to state that determines whether a business is considered "doing business" in that state for taxation purposes.

Domestic Corporation — A corporation formed in your home state.

Employee Benefit Trust — A trust set up for the benefit of employees. The monies placed in these funds are considered an expense to the corporation and taxes are not due on these monies until withdrawn by the individual employees. Normally used with qualified plans such as Keoghs and IRAs and run by insurance or investment professionals as custodians for the corporation. These trusts can be developed with non-qualified plans that remove many of the restrictions of qualified plans. They can be revocable or irrevocable.

Employee —An individual hired by a business to fulfill the common duties of the business through an employee contract.

Employer Identification Number — A number assigned to a business that hires employees, also referred to as an EIN. This number helps the government track and monitor employers. A sole proprietor or partnership may substitute a Social Security number when there are no employees. A corporation must have employees to exist.

The above definitions are not intended to be complete legal definitions. If a full definition is desired, please contact us and we will refer you to a qualified source.

Because a corporation is not able to perform any functions without employees, there must be employees in any functioning corporation.

Expenses — The monies used to pay for anything necessary to transact the business of a company.

3

Fiscal Year — The tax year of any organization.

Foreign Corporations — A corporation that is formed in another state or jurisdiction that qualifies to do business in your state.

Formalities — The procedures that must be followed to allow a corporation to run as a separate entity.

Fraudulent Conveyance — A transfer of property intended to place assets out of reach of rightful creditors.

Freestanding Resolution — A motion passed on the spot by the Board of Directors to resolve an issue. The ability to make freestanding resolutions is given to one director, or there is only one director to make the resolution. This is a more expedient and less formal way of making major decisions in a corporation. These freestanding resolutions still need to be entered into the corporate minutes as past business of a corporation for the next meeting of directors.

Judgment — A motion passed by the courts that legally acknowledges a debt.

The above definitions are not intended to be complete legal definitions. If a full definition is desired, please contact us and we will refer you to a qualified source.

3

Lawsuit — A motion brought before a court to receive a judgment to recompense an injured party for perceived damages.

Legitimate Business Purpose — The reason for existence of the business, which must be legal and necessary to meet the business goals of the company.

Liability — The amount of assessable responsibility involved in any given transaction should there be a loss.

Limited Partnership — A partnership formed between individuals where less than the whole partnership manage or have an effect on the profit or loss of the whole partnership.

List of Officers and Directors — A list filed annually with the Secretary of State that gives the names and addresses of the directors and certain officers of a corporation.

Medical Reimbursement Plan — Money that is set aside for the health benefits of the employees of a corporation. It can be deducted as a business expense.

Meetings — The formal method through which stockholders and directors manage a corporation.

Minutes — The written record of the activities that take place in meetings.

The above definitions are not intended to be complete legal definitions. If a full definition is desired, please contact us and we will refer you to a qualified source.

Nominee — A person selected to handle an office for a corporation, usually an outside person. Commonly used for privacy purposes in a corporation by hiring nominees for all positions that are required to be named on the Annual List of Directors and Officers.

3

Non-Voting Stock — A class of stock that holds no voting power.

Officer — A person appointed to act as an agent of a corporation.

Paper Trail — The physical evidence of the line of reasoning in any business. For example, memos that cause a subject to be brought up in the recorded minutes of a meeting, that causes a motion to be brought before the Board of Directors and voted upon, that causes a resolution to be passed, that causes an action to be taken.

Partnership — An agreement between two or more individuals to work together towards a goal.

Pass-Through Income — The profits paid to the owners of any non-taxed business entity.

Personal Service Corporation — A classification applied to corporations that provide certain services. Personal service corporations are taxed at a flat 35%, without any graduated rates.

The above definitions are not intended to be complete legal definitions. If a full definition is desired, please contact us and we will refer you to a qualified source.

3

Perfection — The method through which a lien on property used as collateral for a debt is recorded

Pre-emptive Rights — The ability that can be given to stockholders to have first rights to purchase a percentage of any stock offered for sale by a corporation in an amount equal to the percentage of the outstanding stock they currently own.

Professional Corporation — Most corporations providing professional services which require state licensing in order to transact business.

Promissory Note — A document that evidences a promise to pay.

Proxy — The ability to act in the place of another. A method used to allow another to vote in your place.

Registered Agent/Resident Agent — One who is readily available for service of legal process. Also holder of Stock Ledger Statement and certified copy of corporate bylaws. Duties vary from state to state.

Registered Shares — Shares that have been issued and the current owners names and addresses are recorded.

The above definitions are not intended to be complete legal definitions. If a full definition is desired, please contact us and we will refer you to a qualified source.

Resolution — A written consent to action by the Board of Directors.

Security Interest — The rights that a borrower gives a lender to seize and dispose of the borrower's property if the debt is not repaid.

3

Security Agreement — A document that sets out the terms of the security interest lists and describes the property involved, and tells when the leader can take it and what can be done with it.

S-corporation — A corporation that meets federal guidelines and has filed Form 2553, Sub-Chapter S Status, which generally affords the corporation pass-through tax treatment like a partnership.

Share Scrip — Portions of a share of stock in a corporation. There is usually no voting power associated with scrip. This scrip may be held in bearer form. Some states have special rules and limitations for the use of scrip.

Shareholder — An owner of stock in a corporation.

Shares — The amount of ownership of a corporation's interests is conveyed in the form of shares or stock in a corporation.

The above definitions are not intended to be complete legal definitions. If a full definition is desired, please contact us and we will refer you to a qualified source.

Sole Proprietor — A business organization where in an individual human being owns and controls a company or business enterprise.

Stock Ledger Statement — A formal way of tracking the registered owners of stock in a corporation.

Subordination — The ability to give another lienholder your position of priority on secured property. Useful in allowing a business in debt to you the ability to secure financing or credit.

Tax Avoidance — Legally structuring your affairs in such a way as to reduce your tax liability.

Tax Evasion — Any action done to circumvent the ability of taxing authorities to receive legitimately owed taxes.

Third Party Transactions — "Arms length transactions" that would occur in the normal course of business.

The above definitions are not intended to be complete legal definitions. If a full definition is desired, please contact us and we will refer you to a qualified source.

Summary

You have probably learned the value that properly implemented strategies hold for you. Remember the three rules:

1. You must have a sound and legitimate business purpose for implementing the strategy.

2. You must completely document the purpose, the action and the timing of the strategy.

3. You must insure that all criteria necessary to allow you to implement the strategy are met and maintained.

Following is a step-by-step task list to help you put your personal version of the Warbucks/Red, Inc. strategy in place and start realizing the fantastic benefits it offers as soon as possible.

Call 1-800-648-0966 where one of Laughlin Associates' experienced consultants can help you build a custom strategy.

■ Warbucks/Red, Inc. Task list

1. Form an S-corporation or an LLC in your home state.

2. Form a regular C-corporation in a state with lower state taxes that has a more business-friendly environment. Best choices are Nevada or Wyoming.

3. Insure that the C-corporation has the ability to hold out to do business with all of the criteria necessary to maintain the corporation's good standing.

4. Process all of the paperwork necessary to perfect the debt(s) between your Warbucks corporation and your Red, Inc. corporation.

5. Follow-up on the strategy on a regular basis to ensure its success.

CHAPTER 4
LIMITED LIABILITY COMPANIES

4

LLCs—The Basics

Traditionally, businesses have taken the form of sole proprietorship, partnership, or corporation. In the past several years, however, all 50 states and the District of Columbia have adopted laws permitting the creation of a limited liability company, or LLC.

4

While relatively new to the United States, the LLC has been the most popular and predominent form of organization in European countries for hundreds of years with good reason. The LLC combines the best features of a corporation and a partnership, and it possesses strategic advantages over both. Like corporations, LLCs shield their owners from personal liability. At the same time, the LLC is entitled to be treated as a partnership for tax purposes and therefore carries with it the "pass-through" tax benefits regular corporations don't have.

The LLC is based upon a very important and respected principle in America called the "freedom to contract." This means that the "members" (the owners of the LLC) are free to agree among themselves how the company is to be run and this agreement or contract will then be upheld in the courts. When you combine this principle with the fact that no member is personally liable for acts of the company—and add to this that profits or losses are passed directly through to the members to be taxed at their individual rates—it is easy to understand why the

LLC is quickly becoming the entity of choice for many business organizations.

■ Organization Of LLCs

An LLC is created by filing Articles of Organization with the Secretary of State. The Nevada LLC statute requires the articles of organization to list one or more managers or, if there are no managers, one or more members. Further, the statutes state that "at all times after commencement of business by the company, the company must have one or more members." The old law required at least two members. This change now allows a one-member business to enjoy the benefit of limited liability, without having to conform to the more rigorous requirements of a corporation.

■ Tax Treatment Of LLCs

Current Internal Revenue Code requires that an LLC with at least two members (owners) automatically be classified as a partnership for tax purposes. An LLC with only one member (owner) is automatically classified as a sole-proprietor for tax purposes. However, the IRS has a provision for LLCs which allows the company to "elect" to be classified as a corporation for tax purposes if such tax status is desired. This election is made on Form 8832.

■ Management By Managers Or Members

The management of the company may be conducted by one or more managers, whose name(s) and address(s) must be stated in the Articles of Organization. Managers may be elected annually by the members (owners). If the LLC is managed by managers, not members, the managers can contractually bind the company. LLCs can also elect to be managed by the members.

4

■ Operating Agreement

The operating agreement should provide the details of operating the LLC and provisions for the distribution of income, gains, losses, and capital during the life of the LLC and upon dissolution. An operating agreement contains many of the provisions present in a good partnership agreement.

■ Member's Ownership Interest

The contributions to the capital of an LLC can be in the form of cash, property, services, a promissory note, or some "other obligation to contribute cash or property or to perform services" (NRS 86.321).

4

■ Transferability Of Interests

Although interests in LLCs are considered personal property, the statutes state that the articles of organization or operating agreement may prohibit or regulate the transfer of a member's interest. Unless specifically provided for in the articles or agreement, a person to whom a member's interest is transferred has no right to participate in the management of the business, nor in the affairs of the business or even to become a member unless a majority of the other members approve. This language suggests that although it is possible to sell interests in an LLC (often a desirable option), the transferability is wisely limited to provide some control over whom the existing members will have as business associates. Current statutes provide immense flexibility.

■ Distribution of Profit And Loss

For any reason that the members decide makes good business sense an LLC that has chosen to be taxed as a pass-through entity may decide to distribute the profits and losses of the LLC in a manner not consistent with the contribution percentages of each member. Thus, if two members of an LLC invest 60% and 40% respectively, they may decide to split the profits or losses of that LLC 50/50 or 70/30, provided they have a good business reason. This division may change from year to year.

■ Withdrawal Of Capital Contribution

Once a member has made a contribution to capital, the members cannot withdraw the capital from the LLC until: 1) all liabilities of the company (except the liability for the member's contribution of capital) have been paid; and 2) other members consent to such capital withdrawal; or 3) the articles are canceled or amended to allow the withdrawal.

■ Your Investment Entity

The LLC is the business entity of choice for investors because of an LLC's pass-through capability and ability to hold passive investments such as dividend-producing stock and rent-producing real estate without being reclassified as a holding corporation (which would increase your tax liability).

■ Indemnity

Many state statutes contain provisions allowing an LLC to indemnify its members and managers in statutory language that is quite close to that contained in corporation statutes.

■ Caution:

A potential problem with LLCs is that there is no uniformity among statutes of the various states. Moreover, LLCs are so new that there is little or no case law interpreting those statutes.

The prudent entrepreneur should investigate the laws of the state where his LLC will operate to determine how the company will be taxed, as well as treated in non-tax matters. The future of LLCs is bright, and it may be helped by a growing desire in many states to enact uniform laws regulating them.

It is likely that absolute uniformity will never be achieved. The growing acceptance and use of LLCs does promise, however, that the states will pay more attention to them, hopefully moving toward more consistent treatment.

■ Summary

LLCs are an attractive business entity for many reasons. The LLC if structured properly, allows its members to receive the benefits of being taxed as a partnership while limiting their personal liability, similar to shareholders of a corporation. The LLC avoids the limiting restrictions of an S-corporation. It protects its members from debts of the company better than the limited partnership protects its limited partners.

The LLC allows its members to participate actively in management without losing their limited liability. The LLC has not yet been tested in many courts, however, and should be used very carefully.

LLCs Versus S-Corporations and Limited Partnerships

4

- With an S-corporation, revenue and expenses flow through to the shareholders in nearly the same fashion as revenue and expenses of a partnership flow through to its partners. Although taxed similarly LLC's have several important advantages over S-corporations.

- S-corporations are limited to no more than 75 shareholders. There is no limit on the number of members in LLCs.

- Shareholders of S-corporations can be only U.S. citizens, resident aliens, estates, certain trusts, or certain qualified tax-exempt organizations. There is no such limitation with LLCs.

- S-corporations can have only one class of stock. LLCs are not so limited. (Note: warrants, options, or certain debt instruments might be deemed a class of stock and cause loss of "S" treatment.)

LLCs vs. Limited Partnerships

A LLC has two major advantages over a limited partnership: 1) none of the members need be exposed to liability; and 2) all members may participate in management of the company while still retaining limited liability.

- Members of an affiliated group are not eligible to become S-corporations. There is no such restriction for LLCs. LLCs can control corporations and have corporations as members. While an S-corporation can own a C-corporation, an S-corporation may not have a C-corporation as a shareholder. An LLC has no such limitation.

- S-corporations must make and file an election with the IRS to become an S-corporation. There is no such requirement for LLCs.

- An S-corporation's election is terminated whenever the corporation has excessive passive income, from either prior C-corporation status or current earnings, for three consecutive years. There is no such restriction for LLCs.